They're Coming for You: Threats and changes from innovative ideas

by

Gareth Little

Thanks to:

Harry Campbell at TheRideshareGuy.com for additional Uber research
Alon Rodovinsky and Ivan Popov of Audio Insurgency

Foreword

It is now completely redundant to begin a book that concerns technology in some way by stating 'the Internet has changed society more than any other invention in the last 50 years!' We are all aware of the huge impact it has had. It is now too late for conversations about whether it is good or bad; if is an invasion then it has happened and we are already pod-people. All we are capable of doing now is talking about how we can either try and adapt to the new world that has been thrust upon us, or try and control it in some way. As the test subjects of a huge, all-encompassing experiment it is up to us to either give the next generation the confidence to embrace the online world or warn them of the dangers that shiny, new things can pose.

It isn't hypocritical to care about the environment and also drive a car, or care about animal welfare while also eating meat. We can all understand that the realities of modern life mean that we may need to use products and services while at the same time wishing that they were better. When enough consumers care about the environmental or health impacts of using a product, either the manufacturer will respond to their demands or another will step in who will.

Awareness of unwanted effects led to the introduction of the Prius and dolphin-friendly tuna and the removal of asbestos from buildings and lead from paint. Both consumers and the watchdog organizations which represent them must be vigilant and ensure that companies are keeping to their promises, since they are masters of semantic manipulation, as many an 'outdoor-reared' pig will attest to.

Being skeptical of the myriad changes the emergence of the Internet has brought about doesn't mean we should all keep a well-maintained roost of pigeons in our gardens for sending messages. We can use the Internet while at the same time wanting it made better. The tricky part will be properly overseeing those new companies which owe their massive reach and impact to technology made possible by the Internet, but which are interested primarily in reshaping the physical and not the online world.

This book seeks to explore the ways in which the largest tech companies operating today are changing the world and affecting the lives of everyone on the planet, whether they realize it or not. It will look at the disregard demonstrated for labor laws and the adherence to the notion that everything is broken and technology is the only cure. It will also discuss the encroachment of technology and the coming inescapability, the lack of choice, of using online services.

Because of the malleability of the terms used to describe modern tech-based companies, they are used interchangeably in this book. The term 'startup' is applied broadly to a whole range of different businesses. While it should actually only refer to temporary ventures which are seeking to create a new scalable business, it is often used to describe any young company. Here, we will talk mostly about startups and new tech companies so anytime an entity isn't directly referred to by name, it refers to both.

1.1 Bringing you together, through us: the sharing economy

One of the most important things the modern generation of tech based startups has been able to do, and one of the most discreet, has been to co-opt, exploit and near enough completely re-purpose the word 'sharing'. It is included so commonly in any mention of services such as Uber, Airbnb and Taskrabbit that readers probably don't even register its presence. 'Share' however is problematic in that context, this positive, caring, selfless word. Barked at children from the time they first grab another's toy until they are old enough to buy something for themselves, it represents a feeling of fairness and co-operation, empathy and community. It is now used as a way to make palatable levels of profiteering and capitalism undreamed-of by even the most ardent industrialist.

Though large and small companies exist to try and make money from matchmaking customers and providers in practically every field imaginable, it is best to focus on the real giants of the industry. It is here that we can see most clearly the effect on the world around us and the possible threat posed by the ambitious people in charge.

The notion of 'sharing' began as a result of a now-famous talk by Rachel Botsman at a 2010 TedXSydney event. She put forward an easy to understand but perhaps naive scenario: the power drill, an object a great many homeowners possess, is only used for around 12 to 15 minutes in its lifetime. She questioned the need for everyone to own a drill and suggested that it made more sense to hire one for the brief time it takes to make a few holes, and if you owned one you should rent it out and make a bit of money. She called this 'collaborative consumption' and it is interesting that money is mentioned right off the bat because somehow, between changing from 'collaborative consumption' to the 'sharing economy' the message became that you should be doing these acts for the benefit of your neighbors. This is what lets the middlemen charge money and claim that it is purely to 'keep the lights on'.

At this time, several startups based around the same concept were already in existence, but the drill story really gained traction and brought the idea to the media's attention. Suddenly many were sure that we would be perpetually lending and borrowing things from our neighbors, meeting people along the way and building stronger, better communities, the only negative side effect being drill makers losing their jobs.

Of all the sites live at the time of this presentation or created shortly after, Ecomodo, Share Some Sugar, Crowd Rent, NeighborGoods, Thingloop, Snapgoods and OhSoWe, only NeighborGoods still exists today, the others having shut down completely or changed beyond all recognition. When reasons were offered as to why the sites didn't work, they all came up with the same thing; people just don't want to borrow/rent a neighbor's anything. Interest in and membership of the sites were high, but amazingly few transactions ever took place. It seems that the reality of listing multiple objects being available for rent, then entering into a dialog with an interested party in order to arrange a mutually convenient meeting time, was just too much trouble.

The drill analogy was used time and time again, repeated as if it were an amazing piece of perfectly obvious but previously unthought-of inspiration. As became evident, reasonable quality drills can be purchased for such a low price that it almost doesn't make sense to borrow instead of own one. Depending on how you value your own time, you could easily waste a few hours searching the community sites, making contact with someone, arranging a handover time, getting to their place and back and then returning after the job is finished. If you get home at the end of it all and find one more picture behind the door that you forgot to hang then you have to repeat the whole process again.

When the sharing economy is being touted by Time Magazine as one of its 10 ideas that will change the world, it can be difficult for people not in a position of power to speak out against it. Certainly as originally envisioned, the notion made a lot of sense, recognizing that there is wastage in things lying dormant. Better a group of people each share a BBQ grill for the few times it gets used over the summer than everyone buy one and have them sitting idle much of the year. So while they still toss around words like 'community' and 'mutual', it took a group of companies who were strictly about the money to come in and make a go of this concept. Forget lending your ladder to some cheapskate down the street, you can run your own Hilton and Hertz mini empire.

At the top of the tree is the 7-year-old ride-hailing company Uber. The company was able to take advantage of both the rise in popularity of mobile applications and also the GPS technology built in to every smartphone to create a service which let users request rides from private car owners who happened to be in their area. From the driver's point of view, it allowed them to easily monetize one of the main financial drains anyone is likely to own, their car. It has come to represent the face of the disruptive tech innovation sector.

Looking at Uber, which is frequently called a 'ride-sharing' service, we can see that it is anything but. Uber is a monumentally huge taxi company which makes its drivers supply their own cars and pay for their own petrol, amongst a host of other things. The only way to use the word 'share' regarding this company, in its true sense, is with Uberpool, which allows you to share a ride, and cost, with someone else going to the same destination. For the drivers (who have little choice but to accept Uberpool fares) this means smaller earnings.

Uber takes a bigger cut for Uberpool rides and the drivers must do more work (make two pickups in two different places) for the same money. The empty seat in the back of the car is what is being touted as the wasted resource. From the driver's point of view it doesn't matter how many bums on seats he has, since he is charging per mile and not per person. Uber definitely sees this as a wasted resource since they make more money from Uberpool rides. Despite the word 'sharing' being pretty strongly linked with Uber, the pooling service is a fairly recent addition and not available everywhere.

Airbnb is also synonymous with the term 'sharing economy', except this time you have to provide your own place instead of your own car. Sharing implies giving, but here people are just renting out rooms with Airbnb charging both the landlord and the tenant.

Taskrabbit, DogVacay, Relayrides and dozens of others use the term 'share' when they should be saying 'rent' or 'sell'.

If this were just a San Francisco fad for people with too much money then it would be easy to dismiss, but every one of these companies is intent on getting rid of the traditional way of doing whatever it is they have decided to 'disrupt'; Uber wants to destroy the taxi industry, Airbnb hotels. Crucially, each wants to be the only one in their chosen field and are willing to sacrifice both worker and public safety in order to drive the growth needed to keep VC money flowing in long enough to outlast their competitors.

1.2 First past the post: speed of growth

In a 2008 paper of the same name, Erik Brynjolfsson used the term 'Scale without Mass' to describe the ability of the new generation of tech startups to grow disproportionately to their size; a doubling of business doesn't entail a doubling of staff or premises. This leverage they command puts them at a wholly unfair advantage against the companies they seek to replace.

Richard A. D'Aveni's 1994 book titled Hypercompetition puts forward the idea that, given anyone can access the same tools and the same market, it is possible for competing companies to spring up much more rapidly than with the traditional model. It would be practically impossible for me to start a new car manufacturing company on my own - even given enormous amounts of time and money; however, I could in a few hours launch a rudimentary social network with little to no initial outlay.

The arrival of a new car manufacturer isn't a big concern for the major players in the industry; even a potentially disruptive one such as Tesla has found a place in the market. A new ride-sharing service would be a concern for Uber or Lyft, however. It could quickly gain market share and if its terms were more agreeable to drivers, there would be nothing stopping them deleting the Uber or Lyft app and installing the new one.

The evidence is plain to see; any number of 'biggest company' lists will include Google, Facebook, Amazon and others that didn't even exist 20 years ago. In cases such as Google, they have been able to fill a need which also didn't previously exist. Amazon has used technology to entirely reshape their industry and has had the most profound effect on retail and publishing in their histories. It took the business communication service Slack around 15 months to reach a $1bn valuation.

With the rise of the huge chain supermarkets such as Tesco, Walmart and Costco, people complained about the death of small grocers and the homogenized experience of food and grocery shopping.

Instacart founder Apoorva Mehta described physically going to a store as a 'broken experience' and hopes to use an army of non-employees to go shopping for people and deliver their items to their homes.

The demand for growth is fueled by the assumption that the first past the post is the winner, and also a fear of missing out. Investors who turned down the chance to get in on the ground floor of one of the now huge companies are a lot less diligent when spending their money now.

Facebook wasn't the first social media site. In 2006 Myspace registered its 100 millionth account and was at one point the website was more visited than Google. In 2013 it reported 36 million users and has now completely rebranded itself as a more niche music and entertainment-focused site.

Because of the willingness of venture capitalists to invest huge amounts into fledgling companies, often without a solid business model or business experience, startups have been able to artificially exert a disproportionate amount of influence and importance in the market. They tend to follow a similar script. Practically overnight they appear with lofty promises of fundamentally changing whatever sector they have chosen. Lots are written about the company, its founders and its ethos. After several months it will go through what is called a 'pivot'. This is when the company realizes that the egalitarian idea it had in mind isn't viable and they need to change fast, typically by cutting the money awarded to the people carrying out the tasks or services. Several months after that the company will either quietly disappear, or the team will write a lengthy public letter about all the lessons learned and how amazing it was to be able to 'start a conversation' about change in the marketplace.

If these companies were forced to do things the traditional way, that is, without any venture capital, they would see much earlier on if their idea was viable or not.

Part of the problem stems from both the mindset of the entrepreneurs and also their socioeconomic situation. Several startup stories begin with things like, 'I wanted to find someone to do X and realized I couldn't.' Many of the Uber-for-X ideas were created by (and for) people with more money than time, who were willing to pay to have menial tasks done for them. They assumed that people with more money than time would be a natural fit for people with more time than money; however, the experience is always worse for the service provider, since not only are they the one doing the task, but they are also worrying about where their next job is coming from and if they can earn enough to make ends meet.

Most of the companies learned that there are only so many people willing to pay to have everyday tasks done for them. For the rest, it would never even register as an option to start paying for things they do themselves all the time.

Having the services online glosses over the messy but necessary person-to-person interactions needed to accomplish these tasks. It is not as easy as saying, 'I'd pay money to have someone do this.' Many tasks which traditionally involve hiring a contractor are things that people are unable to do themselves: plumbing, electrical work, etc. These jobs require skilled professionals who are able to charge money consummate with their skill level, the complexity of the job and also the time that was spent learning the skill in the first place.

The modern gig economy advertises to people who would like to earn some extra beer money but preys on those desperate for work but unable to secure traditional employment.

The franchise model can be seen as a midway point between wholly-owned companies and those which rely on jobbing 'gig' workers. Brands which franchised themselves were able to shift the financial burden of expansion on to the people who wanted to open a new location. The company would provide materials and training to ensure that all locations offered consistent service. Franchise licenses for big chains can be extremely expensive but for the investor, there is less risk if the brand name is already well established and presumably has a good reputation. A takeaway food shop using the Subway branding and menu would have more immediate traffic than if it were an independent called 'Sarah & Steve's Sandwiches'.

Startup founders like posing for photos against the backdrop of their quirky, kitschy offices. This helps with the narrative that they are motivated purely by trying to bring about meaningful change in the world for the benefit of all who live in it. After you read several of these founders' stories, it is difficult not to feel slightly annoyed at the implication that we all live in such an unnecessarily convoluted world and have just been waiting for these people to come along with a standing desk and some code (and all the millions in VC backing) to fix things. The persuasive myth of startups being purely socially positive entities hides their true nature, that they are no different from traditional businesses in their attitude to the importance of money and profit and if anything, despite the beards and comfortable clothes on display in their offices, they are often far more ruthless operators than the most stereotypical big, heartless corporation. They use data and analytics to a frighteningly precise degree to make completely emotionless decisions which directly affect both workers and customers.

All startups depend on VCs' money. VCs invest for several reasons. Historically, although only a tiny percentage when grouped with all those who didn't, several startups have made it, and made it big. This has created a fear of missing out on getting in on the ground floor of the next Facebook, Instagram or Twitter. Twitter especially was a hard sell in the beginning, difficult for even its creators to explain what it was or why people might want to use it. This set a precedent for putting money into products whose potential benefit may not be absolutely clear.

Venture-capitalists are not risk-averse people; they are willing to invest considerable amounts into ideas for the chance of getting a good return in a short space of time. Even the granddads of the online world are only around 15 years old and have grown comparatively slowly compared to the latest generation, Facebook taking 7 years to get to a $50bn valuation compared to four years for Uber. Both Google and Facebook are well run, profitable companies with an assured revenue stream that is unlikely to dry up overnight. Twitter has been struggling since 2013 and most recently was downgraded by Morgan Stanley in October 2015.

Twitter has become ubiquitous in daily life and is used by many as one of their primary sources of information, especially when urgent news stories are breaking. It can be a more immediate medium than TV news channels (which increasingly rely on just reading tweets on air). It has struggled with growing its userbase, however. The number of careers that have been damaged or ruined by a careless comment on the service has frightened some people away from joining. It is also thought of by many, again mainly due to representation in the press, as a pointless pit of unchecked human venom, hysterical over-reactions and witch-hunts.

A consistent behavior exhibited by modern tech companies is the methods they employ to maximize profits and increase efficiency. Practically all the major players involved in the sharing economy have, sometimes more than once, both hiked the fees that they charge their customers and reduced the amount paid out to workers.

The cost of taking on new freelancers has dropped to practically nothing and there is a seemingly inexhaustible supply of people in need of work or extra money so there is little reason for the companies to try and keep workers on their books. It is probably more of a burden for a small team to enter into a dialog with an unhappy worker and attempt to resolve whatever the problem is than it is to just replace them with someone else.

When Ford was transforming the auto industry with the arrival of both the Model T and the assembly line used to build it, it was a famously difficult time for the workers trying to adapt to these new practices and staff turnover was very high. Ford responded to these challenges by doubling wages, cutting an hour off each working day and striving to hire workers who showed real potential, including people with disabilities who at that time would have struggled to find work elsewhere.

We will explore in this book the comparative lack of a competitive market in the online sphere compared to real world companies. The traditional markets of course do not accept an unlimited amount of rival operations. Between 1920 and 1940, 183 US car makers ceased operations while Ford was producing 50% of all cars on American roads. But one car company could never expect to completely dominate the market. For experienced engineers, cars are (or at least were) easy to reverse engineer and copy. Customers' desire for something new and uncommon would prevent everyone ever owning the same automobile, regardless of how advanced or cheap it was. For a company like Facebook to survive, it has to have a monopoly. It doesn't matter if members of the same family drive different cars but if they are using different social networks then it completely negates all the benefits that these services offer. For the social media market to be truly competitive, Facebook would have to be forced to allow other services to be able to communicate with its own users.

Ford was started proper with a $28,000 investment from several backers (around $700,000 adjusted for inflation). This seems an absurdly small amount when compared to the seed capital that today's startups routinely raise. Instacart's second round in 2012 secured it $2.3m. Over the next three years it went on to get $8.5m, $44m and $220m. It claims to be profitable today only through the most creative interpretation possible of its revenue figures and is actually still losing money.

Sometimes pivots genuinely help a service improve. In the early days of eBay, bidding was a lot of fun as in the mind of the customer, it was as close as they were ever going to get to being a mysterious and wealthy international jet-setter, sat in the front row of a Christie's auction, bidding on Fabergé eggs. People would bid then obsessively check the auction page, watching the seconds tick down, trying to create psychological profiles of their opponents based on nothing but screen-names, wearing out the f5 key refreshing the page endlessly during the final 60 seconds. After few auctions though, the emotional turmoil became too costly, not to mention the time involved. It seemed a waste to wait four or five days for something just to lose it by 50p at the last second.

Ebay introduced the 'buy it now' feature and everyone was much happier. Behind the scenes, the introduction of the bulk listing tool for sellers threatened to upset the cart even more. Given a way to quickly and easy list hundreds of products at a time, quality nosedived correspondingly and now you must be much more specific with your search queries unless you want to spend the day looking at page after page of seemingly identical mobile phone covers and ink cartridges given a unique listing for every printer model manufactured since the Gutenberg press.

The consequence of this pivot in the long run, however is with 80% of products sold on eBay now being new, consumers are wondering why they should use the service over any other online retail platform.

One of the best examples of a recent shameless pivot has been Etsy's subtle change from marketplace for handmade crafts sold by the creators straight to the customers to an online marketplace trying to make the word 'artisanal' stick to sweatshop produced goods. Etsy, suffering from the common malaise of slowing growth, realized that there were limited numbers of people with the talent, time or desire to make handcrafted products and sell them online. The solution was to try and reinterpret and redefine what the term 'handmade' actually meant. Now, sellers can resell things that they haven't themselves made. The products can be made in Chinese factories, all that is required is that sellers have investigated the manufacturing process and made sure it isn't too horrible (Etsy themselves take the sellers on their word and do not carry out independent checks).

1.3 Preheat your PC: the death of shopping and cooking

Although it still persists today in various forms, most people are familiar with the reality behind pyramid selling. The illegal scheme, also called multi-level marketing and a myriad of other things, promises a big payment if 6 gullible people can be found to buy something or just hand over cash, but in reality only works for the people towards the top of the pyramid and leaves everyone at the bottom worse off.

The pyramid scheme relies on people's desires to get rich quick but will always be undone by the mathematical impossibility of being able to recruit enough new members to make everyone a profit. The shape, however, can be roughly applied to most traditional businesses, with the majority of workers at the bottom being on minimum wage, then fewer more senior staff on a bit more, managers on a bit more still, area managers, regional managers and so on, all the way to the top. Unlike MLM, this pyramid can be climbed through hard work and promotion.

Taken at their most severe interpretation, several of the big players in the tech startup world have a business model which eclipses any pyramid scheme in terms of sheer efficiency. Of course, MLM is a scam and these companies are not, but even a pyramid shape suggests the top half doing reasonably well.

A similar model of a company like Uber would show a vast, squat line with a comparatively small dot sat atop it. The line representing the thousands of people contracted to work for the company, and the dot the founders and the very small amount of actual employees on salaries behind the scenes. All money from the workers goes straight to the top of this squashed pyramid, with no ranks of people making progressively more money. Freed from things like stock, warehouses, offices, showrooms, health insurance and pension contributions, tech companies are able to rely on the magic algorithms which are the engines of their business. As long as the server is on they can make money with no other considerable outlays.

The following chart demonstrates why we shouldn't think of these companies as job creators, despite their perceived size. They enjoy a customer/employee (real employee) ratio unheard of and impossible before the smartphone age.

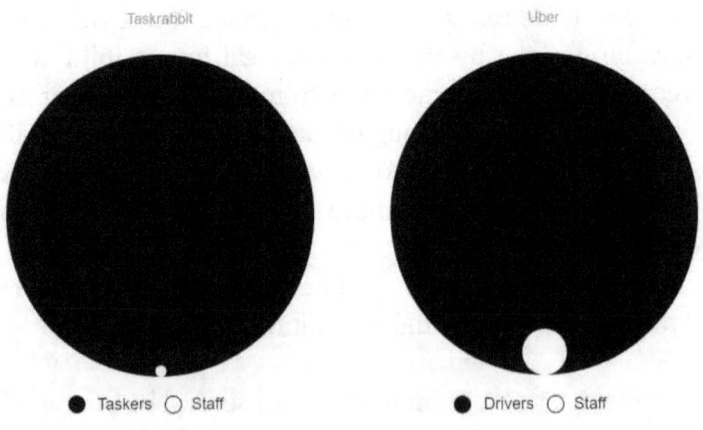

Taskrabbit   Uber

● Taskers ○ Staff   ● Drivers ○ Staff

At the turn of the new millennium, Webvan attempted to enter the home grocery delivery business. To do this it built a string of refrigerated warehouses with automated conveyor belts to load the food onto trucks. Each facility cost between $30-40m. At their peak, they employed 4,500 people to help process the orders in these plants, not unlike Amazon.

Famously, they folded in 2001. Now Instacart and other similar startups are attempting the same thing, but this time using contractors (who pay their own fuel costs) to drive to stores and buy straight from the shelves. They use 4,000 of these contractors and actually employ only about 110 people to work behind the scenes. Despite actually employing only about 2.5% the number of people Webvan did (the significance of employee status is discussed later), Instacart is valued at $2bn, or roughly 33% or what Webvan was at its peak.

Uber currently employs just over 3,000 full-time salaried workers, mainly at their headquarters in San Francisco. Worth around $60bn, it is the most valuable private tech company in the world. These 3,000 employees are sufficient to allow the company to operate in 300 cities in 60 different countries worldwide, managing over one million rides each day. In Wyoming, the least populated US state, the retail giant Walmart employs over 4,600 people, nearly 1% of the population.

Given the right tools and training, it would seem that those 4,600 people could easily control a global business empire with an annual turnover of $10bn, quite possibly alongside greeting customers and unpacking boxes of bananas. Instacart founder Apoorva Mehta said in an interview with Fortune magazine that one of the things they learned while striving for efficiency is that they don't need general managers in each territory, or indeed any managers at the time of launch. The company operates in several locations without having any salaried employees overseeing things.

Although he wasn't the first to make a social network, Mark Zuckerberg still had to create Facebook largely from scratch. Now anyone can setup in a matter of minutes a social network using one of a number of online services dedicated to doing just this. The need to know anything about coding has been removed as an obstacle in the way of making something online. Wordpress, the world's biggest blogging platform, allows anyone to make their own blog without having to enter any HTML at all.

This trend will only continue in the future. Fewer and fewer people will be needed to achieve the same level of impact and results. One of the biggest advancements of these last few years on the Internet has been the rise of Application Programming Interface (API). Among other things, this is a way to use the content from one service in another, for example a technology review website displaying a link to a product on Amazon with a constantly updated price.

Going back to the grocery delivery business, we saw the huge logistical challenge faced by Webvan; they needed a fleet of vehicles and huge processing facilities, all refrigerated, a small army of employees and a constantly-updated website. Now we can make something which achieves the same goal, groceries arriving at a customer's house, but far more simply. Using the Aislefinder API we can very easily plug in constantly-updated information on 150,000 products, including where they are located on 2,400 stores' shelves in the US. So our customers can order though the app and we can push the orders out to our shoppers who will go to the store and do the buying. They'll be guided by the Aislefinder info so they don't have to waste time looking for things. As creators of the app (which we've farmed out to a freelancer) we haven't had to manually enter any product information at all, nor directly employ any staff.

The burden has been completely shifted away from us. We no longer have to have people updating the website with the latest prices of products as that is being done for us. We don't have to have a constant dialog with stores about where their products are located. Our website can come from a template, as can our app. We will hold no stock, own no property and employ no more people than are needed to keep these few things online. We can outsource the hundreds of customer complaints we'll probably receive to a specialist company too.

It is often said regarding Webvan's failure that they were too early to the market with this idea. There were less people online doing less shopping and the idea of having groceries delivered still seemed like an unnecessary luxury.

Launched today, there is every chance that they would operate using a similar model to Instacart. Webvan, however, spent its money on buildings and equipment. It paid salaries to its workers. Construction workers and delivery van companies benefited from its existence as did the companies which supplied the refrigeration equipment. Ultimately it became just like a supermarket, although one that shoppers couldn't visit in person.

Instacart is in some ways a hugely inefficient service. Whereas Webvan bought in bulk (paying wholesale prices) and separated things out in its distribution centers, Instacart shoppers go to the supermarkets and buy things like any normal member of the public would do. The shoppers aren't, however, making the many hundreds of small decisions that typical shoppers do on a trip to the store, they are just there to fulfill a list. So for the supermarkets to go to the trouble of creating attractive displays and highlighting special promotions is completely wasted on people using Instacart. It also involves an extraordinary amount of legwork on the part of the shoppers who, although knowing where everything is, still have to trundle round with a cart perhaps multiple times a day getting everything off the shelves.

Increased use of shoe leather isn't one of the things which concerns a company like Instacart however, since it is the shopper who is putting in the effort of walking around the stores and they are incentivized to do it as quickly as possible so that whatever they earn for doing the task looks more attractive when compared to how long they spent doing it. One metric the company is very interested in is 'items per minute', how many things the shopper can put in their cart in 60 seconds.

As unfair as the above diagram of the modern tech company looks, it may seem positively inefficient in a few years, when extremely small teams will be able to achieve similar or better results using off the shelf solutions. Tech companies hate having employees. Some of the smaller ones will fold rather than bestow employee status on the people doing the leg work for them, while the bigger ones will happily spend untold millions in the courts trying to keep people classified as independent contractors.

Uber has been on a hiring spree recently, but the people it has been hiring have been tasked with one day eliminating the need for the freelance 'driver partners' that bother the company by asking for things like benefits and salaries. The company has launched an advanced technology center in Pittsburgh, where it is researching among other things autonomous, driverless cars.

Unfortunately, just because anyone can make a social network or on-demand app doesn't mean anyone can be the next Silicon-Valley billionaire. There is a startling lack of real competition in the tech world and certainly no room for several companies offering the same service. To win against another startup using the exact same tools and resources we will need lots of startup money so that we can wage a war of attrition and just wait for our competitors to exhaust their resources.

If Instacart wants to form a parasitic relationship with supermarkets, taking advantage of the infrastructure that someone else has paid for and established, other startups want to act more as viruses, killing off the host altogether. While convenient for the customer, supermarkets (if managed badly) can be monumentally wasteful. Getting the same range of foodstuffs onto the shelves of thousands of stores around the country relies on a complex supply chain. Raw ingredients are spirited away from the area they were grown in and sent to huge processing factories. Processing involves some attempt to lengthen the lifespan of the product, so chemicals and preservatives are added, neither of which are necessary or beneficial to our diets in large quantities.

Once finished, the food products are then sent out to distribution centers dotted around the country before finally being delivered to each store. A shockingly large amount of food dies en route, however, and never sees the store shelf. Either due to improper transportation, incorrectly-controlled temperatures or simple human error, millions of pounds in weight of food is wasted before it has a chance to be bought. Add to that the huge amount of food purchased and then thrown away each year, a problem some attribute to excessively generous in-store promotions like buy one get one free and it is easy to see why a new generation of companies want to harness the power of consumer-owned smartphones and GPS tech to try an offer an alternative route from field to plate.

Farmigo is attempting to create a more direct connection between producers and consumers. Farmers, bakers, cheesemakers, etc. input the expected yield of whatever it is they are making in the system a short time before the customers come online to buy, usually about a week before pickup. The customers shop as they normally would. The products are processed in a network of small facilities, where they are separated into each customer's order. Vans then take the orders to pickup points, typically some convenient location (e.g. a school or community center), the customers then come at the arranged time and collect their order.

The company boasts higher rewards for the producers and many more local foods available for the customer. By invoking the word 'community' again, it has managed to convince people to take responsibility for organizing and hosting the pickup locations (organizers get a discount off their shopping). So not only has it offset the costs associated with having their own pickup locations, organizers are giving up their time to hang around waiting for customers to come and collect their orders. Of course, accurately predicting yields for crops is never going to be 100% successful, so customers have to be prepared for what they eventually get to be different from what they ordered in certain cases. Groceries will also be charged at a higher price than in the supermarkets, who are able to command large discounts for volume buying.

Although the system seems simple on paper, both Farmigo and other similar companies are still struggling with scaling. Selling more than they are eventually supplied with is one problem, while certain areas may naturally lack a sufficient variety of different products to make the endeavor worthwhile. Farmigo relies on being able to find good quality volunteers, since they are technically going to be the face of the company when the customers get their groceries. It is demonstrative of the power of concepts such as 'community' and 'neighborhood' that the company can use volunteer labor. Good Eggs required suppliers to take their produce to the drop-off centers at their own expense; there seems to be no minimum order involved so producers have reported having to make the trip just to deliver a single item. As we've seen in other sectors, the grocery disruptors similarly want to keep things at arms- length while also exerting as much influence as they can over things without being held liable. Farmers have been asked to grow certain crops and take on extra staff; like anyone else involved in the 'on-demand' economy, they've found themselves at the mercy of suddenly changing policies and requirements.

It remains impractical for a farmer to rely solely on services such as Farmigo. Farming requires a large amount of upfront costs which may not be recouped for several months. They simply cannot risk growing acres of vegetables then just hoping that the customers feel like ordering them that particular week.

It is a shame that Farmigo chooses to be so militant about its policies. It refuses to sell foods imported from other countries. This practice seems to unfairly penalize the millions of farmers around the world that rely on the export market for their livelihood. Most exotic fruits are transported by sea, by far the least wasteful of all long-distance travel methods. Farmigo seems to have arbitrarily settled on a maximum distance which foods are allowed to journey. The company has the rather lofty idea of killing off the supermarket, surely impractical given that the average person allocates just 7% of their food budget to vegetables. It also ignores the enormous gains in available time that processed foods have given society.

Both Farmigo and Good Eggs are most popular in San Francisco, and both are having difficulty introducing the concept in other places. Good Eggs pulled out of Los Angeles, Brooklyn and New Orleans. It seems that the Bay-Area may be singularly unique in the attitude of its inhabitants. Thousands of tech sector employees with lots of money, little time and often a staunch adherence to the cults of healthy living and eco-friendliness create a big market of positive reinforcement for these startups which find reality, once they leave California, quite different.

Community-supported-agriculture (CSA) is an alternative system already in place. In this mode, individuals pay money to the farmer at the start of the season, then periodically receive crops as they are harvested. The advantage of this system is that the farmer has to shoulder less of the burden of the initial financial outlay. CSA has been running mainly in the US and Canada for over 30 years. CSA requires trust in the farmer on the part of the consumer, since they are paying ahead on the promise of getting vegetables down the line. For any number of reasons, crops may fail or be of insufficient yield to give everyone a good share. In terms of supply chain efficiency it is difficult to beat, since customers are directly investing in the farm. Farmers like to plan ahead, and the entire futures industry is built on the notion that you can reduce risk by selling a commodity that you don't have yet for a lower price, rather than waiting to sell it after you have it.

Good Eggs and Farmigo will need adequate supply to keep customers happy; if everything seems to be sold out then they will stop using the service altogether. In the same way that Uber tackles the problem of customer wait times by hiring too many drivers, thereby disadvantaging them all, Farmigo will need a large supply of food to meet potential need. The problem of what to do with tons of produce that hasn't sold in the days running up to delivery is left to the farmer. These middlemen are recreating the farmers' market online. Farmers markets are risky ventures for the farmers; they can charge a premium to inexperienced shoppers temporarily caught up in the folksy joy of buying veg from a faux-rustic wagon instead of from the supermarket, but stock may only get one chance to sell. Once the day has come to an end the veg is likely to end up on the compost heap. Farmers using online aggregators may strike it rich if by chance they've been growing acres of Kohlrabi and just before harvest Gwyneth Paltrow endorses it as a magical healing medicine but more likely they'll be left calling round trying to get someone to take large amounts of unsold produce off their hands at knock down prices in the hours before it spoils.

Similar to the way that the phrase 'sharing economy' was taken and applied to almost everything (including Netflix at one point), many farmers who have been involved with the system for many years are watching the term CSA being co-opted by organizations that are only marginally in line with its core principles.

Like other areas that have found their business model being attacked by leaner, quicker startups, the retail food industry should see services such as Farmigo as an incentive to modernize their own process. By using technology more efficiently, they could match the ability to have food transported to more, smaller regional processing centers instead of fewer huge ones many hundreds of miles away. By looking at historical purchasing data they could better predict demand. Customers entering a large supermarket, however, have come to expect a vision of plenty, overflowing vegetable aisles, rich with produce. It may take a change in attitude from consumers to accept more seasonality (and therefore less choice) in what is on offer.

If the thought of spending a lot of time cooking all the fruit and veg bought straight from the field is off-putting, then there are also startups which aim to make your whole kitchen redundant. The online platform Josephine matches people who cook with people who don't. The cooks can sell meals. Customers can see what the cooks are making that week and purchase a meal. They then have to make the journey to the cook's house to collect the food. The cooks are responsible for all the costs associated with making the meal and are free to charge what they like. Josephine takes 10% of each sale.

Both cook and customer have to promise to adhere to a code of conduct, although Josephine stipulates that they are in no way responsible for the quality of the food, the manner in which it is prepared or the legality of the ingredients.

As desirable as it may be, services which rigidly supply only organic or non-GMO foods are selling an idea of the world that doesn't exist anymore. Modern crops have been altered to create higher yields, something that will have to increase still further if the Earth's population keeps growing at the current rate. An organic-only diet will remain the preserve of the affluent; it is just physically impossible to feed 7 billion people on traditionally-farmed crops.

1.4 Whats the wi-fi password? Airbnb moves in

Airbnb, which in just seven years has managed to go from zero to equaling the Marriot hotel chain in size, has also used both its own speed and the slowness of government to bypass regulations which affect traditional hotels and guest houses. Originally created as a way for people to rent out spare rooms to travelers (sharing your home), it has ballooned into something else altogether, ironically something which may even be making people homeless.

The company has been keen to hold onto the image presented to the world in the early days, something along the lines of a couple who have a spare room now that their children have grown up and moved out and are able to bring in some extra money by occasionally letting someone stay over. They enjoy a chat over breakfast the next day, learn a little about each other, then the guest departs and the transaction is complete. The guest probably got a better price than a hotel, more comfort and a more personal service. The hosts got money for something which would otherwise have been sat empty.

Behind this image of fostering new friendships and earning extra money hides the real business, the one that makes up the majority of Airbnb's turnover and the one which brings in a far higher cut of profits than the 'mom and pop' operators. In Los Angeles, two-thirds of the listings are for entire units, that is, properties that are solely being used as Airbnb rentals and have nobody living in them otherwise. This is estimated to make up 89% of the company's profit in that area. Multiple-unit operators, people who list more than one property at a time, account for 40% of Airbnb's US revenue.

Much like Uber, Airbnb has had a dismissive view of law and regulations. Many of its listings are illegal under current rules regarding sub-letting and short-term occupancy. It has also been able to get its users to protest on its behalf.

The use of Airbnb by a resident to make extra money can have an effect on the area as a whole, especially in popular cities such as Paris. Hotels are usually located as near to city attractions as possible and smaller guest-houses are easily identifiable. Airbnb takes the same tourists who would normally enjoy a night out before retiring to their hotel and moves them to residential streets. When the home-owner rents out the entire property and is not staying there at the same time as the lodger, the potential for problems greatly increases.

Many locals complain about rowdy guests making noise late into the night and also worry at suddenly having a revolving roster of strangers living next to long term residents. Each set of guests is obviously there to have a good time, with no motivation to be considerate to people living nearby, and are probably unlikely to ever stay in the same place again.

At the other end of the scale, luxury hotels are complaining of a downturn in business. In Paris, at any one time there can be over 400 properties listed on Airbnb which cost in excess of €1,000 per night. These are attractive lodgings for those able to afford it as they are typically in extremely good areas, wonderfully decorated and also offer a far higher degree of anonymity than a hotel can. French citizens can rent out their properties for up to four months of the year and although they are liable for tax on earnings from doing so, they are exempt from the other kinds of tax which a hotel must pay.

A 2015 report by the Hotel Association of New York City threw around some large figures regarding losses which it attempted to lay at Airbnb's feet: $451m in direct revenue, $1bn in construction and $136m in ancillary losses. The report based its figures on the assumption that everyone who booked an Airbnb room would have otherwise booked a hotel if this service didn't exist. Airbnb points out that the money earned by the homeowners stays in the city, going on things like bills and groceries, whereas a hotel chain may just funnel the money away to their corporate headquarters.

Vitally, guests using Airbnb are not covered by any kind of insurance should they have an accident in a host's property. Much of the news coverage of Airbnb 'horror stories' centered on people renting out their home for the weekend and coming back to find it wrecked by a party. Airbnb offers $1m of insurance to cover damage done to the property by a guest, but not the other way around. Also, what many don't realize is that this million dollars only comes into effect when the homeowner's own insurance has been exhausted. The vast majority of homeowners using Airbnb only occasionally would not be able to make a claim for damage done to their property by a guest as most domestic insurance policies have a business activity exclusion.

It can be difficult to muster large amounts of sympathy for people who go away and leave their home in the hands of a complete stranger who then proceeds to damage the property, accidentally or otherwise. However, there is an impression given that guests have been checked in some way. While the site does offer an ID verification service for guests, this is entirely optional and hosts have to go on social media profiles to make their decisions as to whether or not to accept a booking.

In 2013, a Canadian woman died of carbon monoxide poisoning while staying in an Airbnb apartment in Taiwan. While the company did not accept liability, it did pay her relatives $2m. Journalist Zak Stone published a very compelling piece online after the death of his father at an Airbnb house. His father was struck by a branch which snapped when he attempted to use a tire swing attached to it. The swing had been featured in a photograph used to advertise the property. Some have questioned why Airbnb are willing to send photographers to photograph properties (for free) but are not willing to send people to do basic safety checks, such as those carried out on properties which are to be listed as guest houses. The worry for the company is that this would further open the door to all sorts of potential liabilities in the future and make it more difficult for them to claim that they have nothing whatsoever to do with the hotel business.

Residents can navigate their own property unconsciously, they know which doors stick in the frames and that there is a step between the kitchen and the dining room. Guests staying in these homes aren't aware of these things, as trivial as they may be. Whereas hotel rooms are designed with both comfort and safety in mind, the safety aspects being mandated by law, private homes aren't required to have any safety equipment, fire extinguisher, carbon monoxide alarm, etc. if the owner chooses not to install them.

Rightly or not, there are assumptions made by guests who use platforms such as Airbnb that they must be above board. Airbnb is a very famous service, so surely it would have been shut down if it were illegal, the logic goes. Few users take the time to fully read and digest the terms and conditions and anyway, saving money is a powerful motivator and can make a user overlook things they may not otherwise. It is difficult to imaging many bookings being made through hilton.com if their website had prominent stickers proclaiming 'we have no insurance!' 'none of our rooms meet any safety standards!' 'we aren't legally allowed to rent this room to you (but we will, then pay no tax)'.

As with most other platforms which connect service providers and customers, most of the legal burden is offloaded from the company and onto the users. Most sites go to great lengths to make clear that they are just technology companies, not hotel/taxi/cleaning ones. In 2010 Uber changed its name from UberCab to further insulate itself from the regulations placed on the taxi industry. Airbnb describes itself as a 'trusted community marketplace'.

For Uber drivers who are making a bit of extra money on the side, the large group who clock less than 10 hours a week, it can be difficult for them to put themselves in the position of the person driving a cab 12 hours a day who is now taking home less and less each week. Similarly it can be hard for homeowners hosting the occasional paying guest to imagine themselves as part of the same system causing spiraling rents and evictions.

Both these groups of people represent the ideal user of the respective services. These are the people who will happily answer the rallying call when they get a message from Uber or Airbnb telling them about possible legal action which will significantly impact their ability to make money. Nowhere at the protests are the people who own multiple units who are illegally subletting them exclusively on Airbnb, at least not visibly. In some areas, recognizing that the hosts weren't doing it, Airbnb has started collecting hotel taxes directly which can then be paid on to the government.

Stories abound online of tenants being evicted from apartments which subsequently become full-time Airbnb properties. In San Francisco, evictions rose 13% between 2012 and 2013. Landlords employ a variety of means to evict tenants. One of the most powerful in the US is the Ellis Act. This allows a landlord to mass evict all the residents if either the landlord wants out of the property game, or intends to demolish the building and replace it with another. At the end of 2013, a group of tenants were evicted from their complex under the Act, then quickly found their old apartments for rent on Airbnb, at prices nearly 7 times what they paid in rent. This group has launched legal action against both their former landlord and Airbnb itself.

Whereas some landlords have evicted tenants to use Airbnb, and some have evicted tenants for using Airbnb, a third group is actively trying to partner with the company in a move which would allow tenants to rent their properties in exchange for a slice of the profits. From a landlord's perspective this is an attractive proposition since, although they can get more money through Airbnb guests than from rent, it is impossible to predict demand and they earn no money during times of vacancy. Having a tenant would guarantee them a monthly income and then whatever Airbnb commission would be a bonus.

It remains to be seen whether, at its worst, this may be used as a threat against tenants: either stay in your home and join Airbnb or get out altogether. In a block of 20 apartments, how much pressure will be exerted on those tenants who don't want to rent out their places? In popular apartment blocks, it may be that the full-time residents become to the landlords little more than cleaners and security guards, ones who are paying a monthly fee to keep the Airbnb rentals clean and safe. It may also become difficult for residents to bring complaints to their landlord about the behavior of neighbors' paying guests if that landlord is on a percentage.

Airbnb, like all other online services, is a data-driven organization and you can be sure that they keep and analyze the enormous amount of information generated by the millions of transactions they facilitate every year.

When it comes to sharing this data with interested parties, however, they are very reluctant to do so, even if the information has been anonymized. New York State Attorney Eric Schneiderman had to subpoena Airbnb to get it to release rental data as part of an investigation. His findings mirrored those of investigations elsewhere, namely that the majority of Airbnb's profits come not from individual homeowners with spare rooms, but from professional operators who had multiple listings on the site, one man having over 200 apartments to his name. In Los Angeles, a study found that 89% of the company's revenue came from professional landlords or agencies. The same study also concluded that Airbnb had been responsible for taking 7 years' worth of affordable housing off the market, at current construction rates.

Paris lost 20,000 apartments between 2010 and 2015, while becoming Airbnb's biggest market.

The evidence suggests that in normal residential areas which have sufficient housing already, Airbnb can operate with no significant impact. In major cities, which are often perpetually short of housing, the presence of Airbnb makes the housing market much worse, from a tenant's point of view. Landlords seem easily seduced by the thought of bringing in two or three times a day what a full-time tenant would pay, and probably with fewer headaches.

As was the case with Uber, city officials have been extremely slow to react to the appearance of Airbnb and in some areas turned a blind eye to years of law breaking. In Europe, where they are less enthralled by Silicon Valley money, things have progressed further. Berlin enacted legislation banning short-term rentals without prior approval. After Barcelona fined the company €30,000 for breaching tourism rules, the company said that, 'Barcelona should stay on the cutting edge of innovation, and we're disappointed to see a ruling that affects a number of companies and that will hold the city back.'

Companies such as Airbnb and Uber have realized the power of using their customers as lobbyists and protesters on their behalf. When assembled in great enough numbers, their words can carry more weight with those in charge than lobbyists, since the crowds supporting the companies are also voters come the next election. The people who rush to lend their support to their favorite startup are often informed only by the material sent out by the same startup and can be incapable of appreciating the reasoning behind the proposed legislation, only that they've been told by the service they use that they will be detrimentally affected and if they want things to remain as they are, they need to get out and make themselves heard. This tactic cannot be copied by the legislators, since they cannot at the touch of a button contact en masse all the users of a particular service.

Airbnb would like people to think that by allowing local residents to earn money off of their spare rooms, it keeps money in the local area. While this may be true for the portion which the host eventually receives (after 6-12% of the rental price is taken and a further 3% of the host's take) the service charge that goes to Airbnb is immediately whisked out of the country and sent to Ireland, which is notorious for hosting some of the world's biggest companies, lured there by its low rate of tax. Once in Ireland, it can be given as needed to two subsidiary companies based in an even more famous tax haven, Jersey. The two subsidiaries are Airbnb International Holdings and Airbnb 2 Unlimited. Jersey has no corporate tax rate at all. The subsidiaries own the intellectual properties (IP) of the business, so Airbnb can make royalty payments to itself, which would further decrease its tax liability. Traditional hotel companies have no way to compete with this kind of creative tax avoidance. Uber's IP resides in Bermuda, which is where much of the money earned outside the US ends up, after a brief layover in the Netherlands.

As the press periodically report on these kinds of schemes and the public gets briefly riled up, governments play another round of tax haven whack-a-mole. Ireland closed a couple of loopholes after the British Government introduced a 'Google Tax' (which Google doesn't pay). One famous loophole is called the 'Double Irish' and looks set to come to an end completely in 2020; already accountants are looking at benefiting from the same setup in places such as Malta and the UAE. It remains to be seen what eventual consequence the release of the Panama Papers will have on the world of corporate tax avoidance.

Innovation means the old rules shouldn't apply, that they were written for someone else. Most of Silicon Valley believes that there is a universe of difference between a computer and a pen and paper, when in reality there isn't. According to Rebecca Smith, deputy director of the National Employment Law Project, they operate just like old-fashioned labor brokers. The United Kingdom's Secretary for Communities and Local Government, Eric Pickles, scrapped laws which placed restriction on homeowners renting their properties on Airbnb, saying 'The Internet is changing the way we work and live, and the law needs to catch up.' But catching up can all too often mean adapting or compromising, allowing what has up until that point been operating illegally. Nobody, it seems, wants to burden the bright young things who are so keen to disrupt everything with the reason for legislation existing in the first place. That would halt the rapid speed of growth and prevent them from reaching their lofty goals, goals that usually talk about something like 'bringing people together', while accidentally making billions of dollars.

Make it, then fix it, as they say in Silicon Valley.

1.5 Not employees, soon not even people: Uber and the taxi industry

The basic formula for creating a startup is to pick an established industry and see if you can leverage the power of technology to do things better. The textbook example of this are the major ride-hailing services such as Uber and Lyft. They seek to replace what is seen as a slow, old-fashioned and needlessly inefficient service, taxis, with a modern, flexible, tech-driven alternative.

That the taxi industry as a whole was ripe for transformation is undeniable. A background service which operated year after year largely out of the public consciousness and with little thought towards reform or improvement. Uber, launched in 2009, has been able to grow into a $60bn business in 7 years and has truly had a disruptive effect not only on the taxi industry but transportation in general, even in countries where it doesn't yet operate.

The way taxi companies operate varies from place to place, but most involve having to purchase a government issued license to operate as a taxi. In most cases, the number of licenses is controlled, partly as a way of preventing too many cars from operating. Drivers have two choices: buy a license outright or rent a car from a license holder, who will get a cut of their revenue. The cost of the licenses ranges from expensive but affordable to far out of the reach of most independent drivers. In Australia the charge varies from $3,000 for drivers in the country to $22,000 in metropolitan areas. In New York the highly-coveted medallions were sold for over $1m in 2014.

Uber's driver-partners must meet a not-unusual minimum criteria to work for them. They must be 21 or over with a clean driving record and be the owner of a 2001 or newer four-door sedan. The vetting process, which is carried out by a third party and has been criticized for being too lax, takes a few days. If successful, they are issued with an iPhone with the Uber app preinstalled. When they want to work they 'go live', then wait for the pickup destination to be displayed on the phone's map.

Customers can see the car on their own map as it approaches. They also see some brief details of the driver including a photo. Payment is made through the app; no money changes hands. After the passenger is dropped off, both parties rate the other out of five stars. If the passenger gets a lower than three star rating, other drivers may refuse to pick him or her up in the future. If the driver gets below 4.2 then they are called in for a meeting and are at risk of being fired.

The driver is responsible for all charges relating to their vehicle, including fuel. The amount that Uber collects varies by area and during promotional times. Currently they are averaging 20%, with some drivers reporting between 25 and 30%. Uber also takes a $1 per trip passenger fare. Drivers pay $10 a month for the data usage of the iPhones. All drivers are classed as self-employed and receive no benefits.

While primarily marketed as an attractive job for people who are perhaps already in some kind of work or study program, Uber and Lyft are a magnet for people who struggle to find typical hourly-wage employment. These are the people who push the driver hour limits (100 hours a week). In New York, Uber moved in February of 2016 to monitor driver hours daily instead of weekly and to implement a maximum 12-hour day. Previous to this, the New York Post reported that some drivers were doing up to 19 hour days.

Historically, the taxi industry was seen as a way for legal immigrants to work hard and eventually save enough to become owner-operators. With licenses in New York going for seven figure sums and banks requiring $100,000 deposits on loans to buy them, this is now seen as virtually impossible. Instead, already-wealthy individuals took advantage of the system by collecting multiple licenses which were then leased to drivers. The license-owners felt they had an excellent investment, something which was dramatically appreciating in value and also bringing in money each day. So for Evgeny Friedman, owner of over 900 medallions, to seek a bailout in 2014 to rescue him from his shriveling investment points to the transformative power of startups which can practically overnight pull the rug out from under the feet of the established players.

It may be difficult for most people to muster much sympathy for Mr.Freidman, who was able to turn the hard work of hundreds of people into a comfortable life for himself. Certainly there should be more efforts made to prevent these kingpins from controlling too many licenses. Drivers are ultimately a bigger victim of the sudden downturn in license value. For decades the drivers and owners have been investing in this system which allowed diligent and committed workers not only a means with which to support themselves and their families, but also an achievable goal in getting their own license. A driver could begin driving a cab, save enough for a deposit on his own license, and pay it off over several years, eventually owning outright this valuable document.

Now a generation of drivers are watching their investment disappear as thousands of casual drivers take to the streets after nothing more than the most cursory of background checks.

New York's fleet of 13,000 iconic yellow cabs have been overrun by approximately 26,000 Uber 'driver-partners'. The state was involved in a long running battle to introduce plans to cap these numbers, but eventually caved in in 2015. Uber reports that in Toronto, where its drivers earned on average $3,125 in the year Sep 14-15, that more than half of its drivers work less than 10 hours per week. One of the main attractions for the driver-partners is the notion of choosing your own hours, but the tens of thousands of drivers working for just over two hours a day on a five day week are doing so for extra money, not as a sole source of income.

Lyft is Uber's main rival and operates in much the same way. Unlike in the traditional setting, where multiple companies can operate in the same market alongside one another, Lyft and Uber are actively trying to destroy one another and dominate the market.

Competition is of course good for the market, driving prices down (to a point) and spurring innovation. In the fast food field, several companies exist who, while obviously aiming to increase their size and market share, are not locked in an ultimately detrimental battle with their rivals.

Both Lyft and Uber are seemingly perpetually involved in legal action regarding both the status of their workers and the status of the companies as a whole. The companies don't want to be called taxi companies and they don't want their drivers thought of as employees. Historically, the primary difference has been that the drivers are using their own vehicles and that all Uber and Lyft are doing is matching them up with people nearby who happen to need a ride somewhere. Incredibly, both Uber and Lyft are now offering to rent prospective drivers cars, should they want to work for them but either do not own a car or have one which meets the minimum requirements. Still, despite now providing the cars, the drivers and the passengers, they still maintain that they are not taxi companies.

This classification of whether or not they are a taxi company may have more of an impact on the public if they were made aware of exactly the kind of taxes that Uber and Lyft are dodging, and what those taxes are used for. In New York, taxes collected from traditional taxi companies are used to help fund the public transport system. As taxis make less and subsequently pay less, it is not impossible to imagine a knock on effect where there is less investment in the public transport infrastructure. This will result in a worse service and experience for the residents of the city, who may then decide to give Lyft or Uber a try since they can no longer get the bus to where they want to go.

In January of 2016, San Francisco's Yellow Cab Company filed for bankruptcy. Importantly, one infrequently-mentioned advantage of traditional cabs over private cars is their ability, and indeed their duty, to pick up and help transport people with mobility problems. Taxis can be mandated by city laws to provide access for disabled passengers. It would be impossible for Uber and Lyft to mandate that private drivers outfit their own cars with similar features.

In 2014, Uber rolled out an officially-sanctioned program called SLOG. Employees would make and cancel rides with Lyft. CNN reported that, according to Lyft, some 5,560 bookings had been made by Uber employees in an effort to waste their driver's time. Employees would also take rides from Lyft drivers, but during the course of the journey, would get them signed up to Uber. Some employees would even travel with the iPhone with which the new driver would be issued immediately on accepting. These recruiters could make up to $750 per new hire.

Both companies were able to use their large reserves of VC funding to try and outdo one another when it came to signing new drivers. Neither company is allowed to make drivers work exclusively for them (because they aren't employees, remember) so large cash incentives were offered. Savvy drivers could for a time make money by allowing themselves to be seduced by both companies, but this would only result in a one-off signing bonus. As well as drivers, both companies want to attract users, and do so by cutting fares. In 2014, Uber cut fares by 20% and commission from 20% to 5%. Four months later, the commission went back to 20% but fares stayed the same, meaning that drivers were worse off than they were before. In 2015, Uber began offering guaranteed hourly earnings for drivers, but to be eligible drivers had to accept 90% of fares, give at least one ride an hour and be available for work for 50 minutes out of every hour. This meant that it became all but impossible for drivers to also be working for Lyft or other services.

Why can McDonalds and Burger King coexist in the same town, in many cases almost on the same street, in thousands of different locations? They don't make large orders for burgers at each other's restaurants then cancel before paying. They don't try to undercut one another to the point of unprofitability. In the case of McDonalds and Burger King, although they both offer burgers, they aren't exactly the same and the menus are quite different from one other.

There are several areas in which they can offer a different experience, price, taste, range, even crispiness of the fries. Uber and Lyft are essentially offering the exact same service. Having someone take you in their own private car from A to B is going to be virtually the same experience regardless of whether it is with Uber or Lyft.

Therefore the only way that they have to distinguish themselves from one another is through price and the perception of convenience. If Lyft users are finding they are waiting too long to be picked up (perhaps because drivers are busy wasting time on fake Uber bookings) then they are likely to give another service a try. Similarly, if they are making the same journey over and over again, they can easily see if one service offers better value than the other.

Taxi firms lack the booking app which is the keystone of the Uber and Lyft business model. Some city taxi firms are rushing to try and emulate this app as a way of clawing business back from the ride hailing companies. The lack of the app, however, helps keep several taxi companies working alongside one another without fights breaking out. Users who need a taxi just flag one down on the street. Unless they've had a particularly bad experience with a company, they probably don't care or think about what firm they are using, they just jump in. It would be very difficult for one taxi company to wage the kind of war that Uber and Lyft engage in. Having users on the street essentially picking a random cab from a pool of companies each time means several operators can work in the same area and each has a fair opportunity to collect passengers. Users of Lyft and Uber are forced to make a choice. There is no common standard amongst the cars or drivers, so they may experience both clean and dirty cars, friendly and unfriendly drivers, so they have little reason to stick with a company for any other reason than price and convenience.

Despite the size and influence of the company, over the long term the Uber business model remains unproven. Uber remains unprofitable and relies on the immense outside funding that it has been able to attract from venture capitalists. The startup scene is littered with the corpses of once-optimistic companies who tried to apply the same concepts to different markets and unfortunately couldn't make it work. Homejoy wanted to provide an army of people who would come and clean your house for you. Cleaners told the now-common story of struggling to make ends meet and by keeping their contractors at arms- length, Homejoy couldn't offer any kind of consistency. Exec wanted to provide minions to do any job but it became obvious that when even niche providers struggle, one as ill-defined as Exec was going to have a very difficult time. Cherry allowed users to magically have their car cleaned while they were at work, no matter where they left it. Prim would dispatch someone to your home to pick up your stinky clothes, take them to the laundry then return the clean ones to you.

The vast majority of these startups are essentially the same company. They only differ in the scope of the service they offer, either doing just one thing like washing your car, or doing practically anything. In most cases the creators seriously overestimate just how big a demand there is for what is basically a butler you pay by the hour. Living in the bubble of San Francisco where many people have more time than money reinforces the belief that there is a market for things like this. Despite it not being a particularly enjoyable task, most people would have a hard time justifying hiring someone to do their laundry for them, or wash their car, or prepare all the ingredients for their evening meal etc.

The ride-hailing companies like to talk about two main benefits of their service over a traditional taxi. The first is safety, especially for female passengers. The user sees a picture on their phone of the driver coming to get them, so when he arrives, they can be sure that he is who he says he is. Also, they pay for the ride electronically, so no money changes hands. Despite dozens of reports of physical and sexual assaults by Uber and Lyft drivers, this concept of safety is an important one and certainly highlighted the problem that many people, both male and female, have when getting into a cab with a driver they don't know.

The existence of these companies should further help efforts to stamp out unlicensed drivers operating as taxis, although both companies have been criticized for the superficiality of their background checks. In the US, neither company runs a background check using a fingerprint in addition to personal details. The FBI estimates that this can result in a 43% error rate. The second reason is that, especially in big cities in the US, there is a long history of complaints from African-American citizens of being unable to get a ride in a taxi, and that they are often ignored when trying to flag one down, or that taxis refuse to come to areas populated predominantly by African-Americans. Uber and Lyft drivers are able to refuse fares if they choose, but only to a certain limit. It is well known that no money changes hands during an Uber or Lyft ride so drivers from both companies should feel safer going to any area of a city.

In April 2016, Uber agreed to pay out $10m to settle a lawsuit brought by the cities of San Francisco and Los Angeles that alleged the company had misled people about the thoroughness of its background checks. The company no longer claims that it has the best background check policy.

Both of these benefits touted by the ride-sharing companies are valid ones and point as much to failings by cab companies as they do to innovation by the new operators. However, both Uber and Lyft are using these problems as validation for their disruption of the entire cab business. Because certain groups of people can't get taxis or don't feel safe in them, is this a justification for such a radical transformation? Change is preferable to destruction and sometimes it can feel like helping alleviate these problems is just a convenient side effect of the emergence of ride-hailing services, which are rampantly capitalist companies engaging in massively anticompetitive practices behind the friendly screen of the 'sharing economy'.

In November 2015 a group of medallion-holders in New York filed a lawsuit against regulators for allowing services such as Uber and Lyft to operate in the city, a move which they say has seen their monthly leasing income drop 50%.

Amazingly, Uber has been able to operate under a 'make it, then get permission' model. They are not only fighting against regulation, but openly flouting it as they do so. From December of 2014 until April of 2015, Uber operated completely illegally in the city of Portland. The weekend after they launched the city filed a lawsuit against them for failing to adhere to regulations. Given the maximum fine possible in this case, $3,750, it is perhaps not surprising that the company decided to press ahead. During the initial period when the city was threatening to fine drivers and impound their cars, the company promised workers that they would pay any fines and to 'uber on'. Their behavior forced through action in April 2015, not on shutting them down or issuing more fines, but on whether to make them legal or not. In that month, they were given permission to operate under a 120-day pilot program. As part of the agreement, the cap on taxi fares was also lifted for the company, which meant that they were able to continue implementation of their 'surge-pricing' policy, where they can increase fares during times of peak demand. This process, like everything else, is done automatically.

This points to a damaging attitude towards tech companies regardless of size, one that they are keen to promote and maintain. Despite the huge profits they make each year and the ruthlessness of their business practices, the companies like to position themselves as plucky underdogs, using tech to take down Goliath and make a fairer society for everyone. These people aren't interested in money, they are on a social mission. They aren't businesspeople because they don't wear suits. They're just a group of people tinkering away in a garage. Business is corporate and cold, they are all about sharing.

When the government or regulators try to make these scrappy idealists comply with established laws designed to protect workers and the general public, they can accuse them of being anti-innovation and out of touch with the fast-moving modern world. To the public, these laws (whatever they may be) must be out of date efforts to keep regular folks from being entrepreneurs.

The speed at which these companies can grow means that before meaningful legal action can be taken against them, they are in a position to protect themselves by hiring lawyers and by getting public backing, since local government will be seen to be trying to take a service away from people who are presumably enjoying using it.

These types of companies have been extremely efficient at outsourcing everything, including their PR. Customers themselves become unpaid lobbyists and advocates for the company. In the US, local governments seem to have been completely blinded to the similarities between ride-hailing apps and taxi companies, instead focusing on the differences and believing that technology separates them more than it actually does.

Spending on public transport has long been a burden for many cities. It is expensive and it is difficult to measure in terms of money exactly how having buses, subways and trams benefits the residents and the city as a whole. While large cities with a huge number of tourists often go to great lengths to provide modern, convenient means of mass transit the daily task of ferrying normal residents around is often more neglected. In the past, Uber has said that it doesn't want to compete with public transport at all, merely supplement it. Even if the majority of bus users wouldn't normally get a taxi, the mere availability of such a convenient mode of transport as an Uber car can be enough to help councils justify slashing budgets.

With one of its latest endeavors, Uberhop, the company is taking another step towards public transport. Uberhop allows a group of people who are going in roughly the same direction to share a ride. The Uber app will direct them to the pick-up point, usually only a short walk from where they are currently located, where they all meet and get in the car. Similarly, the drop-off point will be somewhere roughly the same distance from each occupant's intended destination.

Uberhop is potentially a more troubling service than the normal taxis. A great many people would never normally take a cab except in case of an emergency, for it is simply too expensive; they are entirely reliant on public transport. There is something sad about the idea of a city failing in its duty to provide a basic service such as transport for its citizens, instead forcing them to spend money with a private company. Although bus fares are usually very low, the money collected can still be reinvested into the service to help maintain and upgrade it, but not so with Uber.

Since the Google buses in San Francisco were able to illegally use public stops for years on end without incurring any penalties before being given official permission to continue doing so, there is no reason why Uber won't try the same thing. Several city regulators have given them special treatment despite the protests of taxi companies. Since the people doing the regulating in this case are also the people who are in charge of the buses, there will be no one to organize any kind of meaningful protest.

The danger is not that Uber replaces buses, but provides a viable enough alternative that both investment in and use of buses drops. Fewer passengers means less money available to maintain the fleet and old, unattractive buses may push more people to using a private alternative. If city-wide protests staged by thousands of irate taxi drivers can fail to bring about any kind of meaningful change, then it is very doubtful whether a comparatively smaller collection of bus drivers will gain any traction when complaining about the possibility of losing their jobs.

The Uberhop service launched in Toronto in December 2015 and shortly after the Toronto Transit Commission (TTC) requested that its legal department look into whether the service is in breach of city legislation or not. The City of Toronto Act gives the TTC sole rights to all public transportation, save a few exceptions like tour and school buses. The Toronto Uberhop service runs during the morning and afternoon rush hours, to downtown from several new apartment buildings. Users are charged $5 and are picked up and dropped off from dedicated spots by SUV-type vehicles or minivans.

The city of Toronto had previously filed an injunction against Uber but lost that battle in the courts, with the judge deciding that the company was merely passing messages between drivers and potential passengers. It seems possible that, if the latest investigation ends up in court, Uber may be able to argue a similar case.

Supporters of services such as Uber and Lyft claim that ride-hailing apps increase choice for people and also threaten to break up the taxi monopoly on transport around the city. Calling the taxi industry a monopoly is a mistake as it is not one organization but many, each in competition with one another. Uber is trying very hard to achieve a monopoly. While each new service added, Uberpool, Smartroutes, Ubercommute, is touted as a choice, they are all just differing means to ensure that money ends up in the hands of the same one company.

Naturally, more people sharing a ride means less earnings for the drivers. The flexibility for drivers touted by Uber means that the work has to be done by a larger number of people compared to taxis. Taxi drivers predominately work either full-time, or part-time (evenings and weekends). It is not practical for a driver to just hop into a cab and do a few hours here and there as he or she chooses. With the majority of Uber drivers logging less than 10 hours a week, that means a huge number of potential drivers on any given day. Uber seeks to replace full-time cab drivers with something far less efficient from the driver's point of view, since it is extremely difficult for them to replicate the volume of passengers when working for Uber full-time. A ride which they may normally have claimed could instead go to a driver who is only logging on for an hour of work before doing something else. There seems to be no limit to the amount of driver-partners that Uber would like to have, since it means shorter waiting times for the passengers and they are also not obliged to give any driver a minimum amount of work. This also contradicts the company's PR line that one of its main goals is to help reduce congestion on the roads, when the complete opposite seems to be the result.

For many people, there may be no reason to choose a cab over an Uber, but competing ride-hailing services cannot exist alongside one another in the same way that taxi companies can, so a duopoly or even monopoly is inevitable.

After the very public showdown between Uber and New York Mayor Bill de Blasio, a report was commissioned to look into the effects of ride-hailing services on the level on congestion in the city. In January 2016, after some unexplained delays, it was finally released and it concluded that services such as Uber were not responsible for an increase in the amount of traffic or congestion in the city. The report recommended against enacting a limit on the amount of Uber cars allowed to operate within the city. Immediately after its release, however, the report was heavily criticized for its brevity and also the lack of hard data to back up the claims made within.

Contrasting this with statistics released by the UK's Department for Transport paints perhaps a clearer picture of the Uber effect on a city. Between 2013 and 2015, there was a 25.9% rise in the amount of private hire vehicles operating in London, reaching over 60,000 in total. Uber CEO Travis Kalanick has previously claimed that an

Uber driver reduces the amount of cars on the roads by a ratio of 7.5:1, a figure which has been widely debunked since it seems to assume that every single passenger would otherwise be driving their own car.

In London, although the statistics don't explicitly say so, the rise in congestion does seem to stem from the increased presence of Uber drivers. Car ownership amongst London residents, already the lowest per person in the UK, has been declining year on year since 2001. During the same 2013-15 period, the amount of traditional taxis only increased by 1.5%. The New York report suggested that the presence of Uber cars had been offset by a corresponding fall in the amount of yellow cabs. The London data doesn't match up with this as taxis also increased, although by a dramatically smaller amount. The data suggests that people are choosing Uber over public transport, which is a far more efficient way of moving a large number of people around a very space-limited city.

London has the highest levels of nitrogen dioxide of any EU city. It boasts a very famous and efficient underground and a well-maintained fleet of buses, all of which help shuttle around the enormous number of tourists who flock to the city each year. London is also famous for the steps that is has taken to try and reduce the amount of congestion in the heart of the city and is no longer a very convenient place to drive if you don't have to. There is a high congestion charge in effect during certain times of the day which has previously gone a long way to reducing the number of cars on the roads.

Uber cars, like the famous black cabs, are currently exempt from these charges. The former Mayor of London, Boris Johnson, failed in a bid to introduce sweeping changes, including a cap on driver numbers, which would have had a massive impact on the way Uber operates in the capital. Instead, his office is now looking at making Uber pay the congestion charge. A disproportionate amount of attention is instead paid to the tourist-targeting rickshaws, relatively tiny in number, emission-free but notorious for trying to fleece naive visitors to the capital and driven by operators with scant regard for the rules of the road.

Uber enjoys the free public support of many who use its service. They often rally against plans to introduce limits or restrictions to the service. As a result of the UK having the highest NO2 levels in Europe, the country is facing an annual fine of €300m for failing to reduce the level of this particular pollutant, which has been linked to thousands of premature deaths every year. It is disappointing that, in the capital at least, they are undoing so much of what was achieved in reducing vehicle numbers by allowing a single company to add many tens of thousands of vehicles without paying any sort of compensation at all. Vehicles which threaten both the jobs of full-time taxi drivers and also investment in one of the best city transportation services of any major metropolitan area.

Back in New York, average speeds within the city, which had been starting to edge up after the introduction of more bike lanes, have started to come back down again. Bus use is falling after several years of flat performance. Regardless of what the most recent report said (or didn't), more compelling evidence is on display everytime someone takes to the streets and experiences firsthand how labored progress from A to B has become.

One vital service which taxi companies offer which Uber and Lyft haven't even tried to touch so far is being able to accept passengers who use wheelchairs. Most developed countries have laws requiring taxi companies of a certain size to be able to accept passengers with mobility problems. It is more cost-effective and efficient for private cab companies to be wheelchair-accessible rather than for the city to provide dedicated on-demand transport. The District of Columbia imposed a deadline for companies with 20 or more vehicles which said that 6% of their fleet had to be wheelchair-accessible. The 20 companies which failed to meet the deadline were threatened with closure until they met the minimum standard. This particular law only applies to companies, not owner drivers, which make up 70% of taxis in the District.

One concern is that as taxi business declines in many areas, it threatens the existence of companies which operate wheelchair-accessible vehicles.

As more people use services like Uber and Lyft, it threatens the existence of bus and subway routes which may be scaled back if passenger numbers drop sufficiently. Uber has partnered with Hasco Medical to enable drivers to buy modified vehicles at a discount, but it is unclear how many people have taken advantage of this offer and even at a steep discount, it would take a lot of rides to pay off a vehicle bought almost specifically for working for Uber.

1.6 More money than time: services for sale

The sheer number of people being quickly employed by this new generation of companies perhaps blinded governments, ever keen to reduce the unemployment figure, to the realities of their working conditions. Companies such as Uber are able to defend their position by promoting themselves as job-creators. Recently, a pushback has begun, not only by by workers who have had to endure sudden changes to pay with little or no dialog with their employers, but now by some government ministers who are seeing organizations bragging about their huge growth and profit, but sidestepping things like payroll taxes and other obligations.

One major downside of the Uber model stems from the classification of its workers. To save money, they are hired as independent contractors and are therefore ineligible for a range of things such as pensions and healthcare. It is questionable, however, how these contractors value their relationship with the company. Indeed, they may never physically visit the headquarters or meet an actual employee of the company they work for. This means no sense of loyalty to the company, no feeling of being valued themselves and no hesitation about leaving. Instead of receiving an annual or twice-annual performance review, these contractors are rated after every single interaction with a customer. While the people driving are called 'driver-partners' by Uber, it is difficult to think of them as partners in any real sense of the word. They receive no bonuses, security or benefits from the company. Their pay doesn't increase in line with the company's earnings, they own no stock. Workers can be caught out by not realizing that they are solely responsible for paying their own tax bill and that no money is being deducted towards that. This practice is common amongst all companies operating under the sharing economy umbrella.

In California, where Uber is based, a class action lawsuit is currently going through the courts. Brought by three Uber driver-partners, it seeks to have them classified as employees and reimbursed for the expenses incurred while driving for the company. Drivers who joined Uber after June 2014 signed an agreement preventing them from taking part in class action lawsuits against the company. Judge Edward Chen overruled this, however, allowing potentially 160,000 drivers to join the action. Uber naturally filed appeals against everything it possibly could.

Uber has pivoted again recently regarding how they classify their driver-partners. Amazingly, they are now being referred to as customers, the reasoning being that the drivers are paying Uber for a product, access to the booking platform, which they can exploit in order to grow their own business. This is of course nonsense; the drivers aren't business owners. The best the drivers can hope to achieve is to be busy for their entire shift with no wasted time. They can never grow beyond that since they cannot themselves hire additional drivers and they can never earn more than is possible from this theoretical perfect day.

As well as the overt disadvantages of being a contract worker, if a company ceases business, it does so suddenly and leaves the contracted staff without any severance or income. The people working on the inside, as well as commonly earning six-figure salaries, often quickly move to another company in a similar position. They will hopefully have had more warning of the impending closure of the company, after all.

For the advantage of flexibility, workers put themselves at enormous risk. Now cut off from any sort of unemployment insurance offered by their governments they are essentially always one hour away from being out of work. Depending on the company they may earn no money for several hours at a time and it can be difficult or impossible for them to juggle more than one income stream as they are expected to be 'on-demand' exclusively for one master.

Interestingly, the issue of worker status and staff training are strongly linked. One of the criteria which the government uses to decide whether people are employees or independent contractors is how much control the company has over the people working for it. In the case of Homejoy, they could schedule training sessions but not mandate attendance, nor could they enforce a dress code or even a list of common core standards, instead having to produce more informal guidance booklets and dress up the language such as by saying 'Clients have told us they like it when...'.

With no training offered, housecleaning startup Homejoy couldn't maintain any kind of consistency and lost many customers who were unhappy with the service. From the customer's point of view, they would be unhappy with Homejoy as a whole and would be unlikely to recommend it to a friend, even if they were just unfortunate to have been paired with a not particularly good cleaner.

In all of these services, the people doing the direct hands-on work are the ones who are at the greatest disadvantage. The customer gets a highly flexible, on-demand service, often at a dramatically cheaper cost than through traditional channels. The company gets a slice of each worker's fee for doing comparatively little, since all scheduling and booking is automated. These companies are unique types of middlemen. Homejoy went so far as to boldly proclaim at the top of their terms of service page that they were not a cleaning company at all, merely one offering information by which a third-party cleaner could be hired. They were able to take $10 per hour, every hour, from each worker just for making this introduction.

The founders looked at the traditional model, where employees would go to a central location before being dispatched for the day, and saw something broken. They saw things like time off, insurance and healthcare as old-fashioned obstacles getting in the way of growth.

One glimmer of hope, in an effort to counteract Uber's dominance, and perhaps an admission that they can't do it alone, some similarly-structured ride-hailing companies have begun working in partnership, so one app can be used to summon a car from more than one service. It would be nice if this led to a collection of much smaller companies working alongside one another; however, it also risks turning into a winner-takes-all battle where prices, and subsequently drivers' earnings, will be lowered in order to lure customers.

There is now a 'race to the bottom' feel to these companies, as the more obvious (and likely useful) Uber-for-X businesses are claimed, the rest seem more desperate, forced. Instacart is trying to ignore the story of Webvan, which went through $800m before going bust. These companies are operating under the impression that food shopping is such a horrible chore that people will happily pay someone to do it for them. Pay not only a delivery cost, but also a markup on many items. The profit margin in the grocery industry is notoriously small, about 1.5% in the US.

A key difference is that, with a service like Uber, there may be no alternative for some people. There may be no good or convenient public transport, no taxis willing to come to where they live. Food shopping is something most people can do unaided. In the UK, the supermarket giant Tesco offers home delivery from as little as £1 if you are not fussy about the time. Even they had to increase the minimum spend from £25 to £40 in 2015.

The Uber-for-X companies are able to project an image of massive size by touting figures such as number of orders processed and how many contractors they have working for them. In reality they are offloading everything which costs money onto the people working for the company: transport costs, healthcare costs, infrastructure, etc. Instacart is using the supermarkets as their storage facilities, the shopper's vehicles as their delivery fleet. Taskrabbit boasts that 80% of its workers have a college degree and that they are not low-wage workers. To make ends meet, however, the taskers (the name for the people doing the work), really have to be doing it full-time. It is questionable how valuable to employers a few years of doing paid errands will look on someone's resume.

Initially, Taskrabbit did act as more of a neutral middleman between people looking for work and people who needed things done. The taskers could view a list of available jobs and bid on the ones that they were interested in. This way, they were able to set their own prices and limit the kind of work to what they felt suited them. In 2014 the company abruptly changed their business model (or pivoted) and removed the auction-style system. Instead, each tasker is assigned an hourly rate and is expected to be available immediately. If they are not able to commit to doing a task within 30 minutes of it being offered, then it is automatically offered to someone else. The backend computers automatically handle the process of matching taskers and service users.

The backlash against the changes was very vocal, but a collection of non-unionized non-employees who have never met one another were never likely to force change from within the company. Whereas previously they could bid on a task and enjoy some sort of interaction with a potential client, now the taskers are completely reliant on the mysterious matching process handled by the company's algorithm. Since they cannot see the jobs in advance, taskers have been left sitting at home waiting for the phone to ping, unable to schedule their day, not sure if they will work that day or indeed ever again.

One of the big uses for do-anything services like Taskrabbit is cleaning. Cleaning is yet another of those things that is not terribly pleasant or unpleasant to do yourself. In the past, hiring a cleaner would be a fairly large undertaking, since you would have to find, research and choose a company. You would probably have to commit to either a certain amount of visits or a fixed weekly schedule. Since they would have many other clients you'd both have to agree on a time when it was suitable for you both. It would be a considerable expense since you would be paying not only for the cleaner's time, but also in part for the office the cleaner worked from, their company van, all the cleaning supplies they used, whatever health and safety training they'd been required to undertake and also the insurance that they were mandated to have before setting foot in your filthy home. Now thanks to apps like Taskrabbit, all that has been done away with. You just open the app, tell it that you want your home cleaned, picking whatever time suits you, and that is it. From the point of view of the person whose house is being cleaned, it is extremely convenient and quite probably cheaper than using a traditional cleaning company. What they should keep in mind, however, is that for the convenience and low price, the cleaner must take on an equal if not greater burden of inconvenience, and they must also absorb the difference in cost between hiring a company and an individual.

It has been said that, rather than being innovative, service-for-hire companies are taking advantage of, and reliant on, a weak economy. The scarcer employment is, the more willing people are to accept entirely disadvantageous terms and restrictive conditions. All companies matching workers and employers take some sort of cut. This is for real staff wages and the cost of keeping the all-important servers running. The majority of sites have a purposefully opaque sliding remuneration system which lures people in with promises of high hourly wages and masks the actual take home money. Very few of the workers bother to calculate their actual income once all the various deductions have been made, fuel, materials etc. Few workers also want to confront the truth about an hourly rate of $25 not being so great if they've been sat at home for five hours not earning anything before getting that hour's work.

Most sharing economy startups are at their core just well-managed and maintained message boards dedicated to one purpose. They are wrapped in a nice, user-friendly app but underneath it all are the modern equivalents of the common room notice board advertising refrigerators for sale or requesting long distance ride-sharing. Some, like Taskrabbit in their early days, attempted to cater to any possible request, but most focus on one thing, some to a baffling degree.

Turo, formerly RelayRides, is another company that operates under the term 'sharing' but is actually just renting, allowing people to hire the cars of private individuals when they are not being used, so Airbnb for vehicles really. It launched under the painfully earnest slogan 'for the community, by the community'. Turo takes 25% from the car owner and 15% from the person borrowing. Incredibly, people are willing to pay this concession to be introduced to one another. More incredibly, the company doesn't make any profit. Like most startups in this field, they had to pivot from their original model when they discovered it didn't work, in this case, dropping the ability to rent cars for short periods of time. Now the average rental is a few days or more. So this 'for and by the community' company is now Hertz except they don't have to bother cleaning the cars each time; the owners will do that. Despite a nationwide rollout in the US, they are not welcome in New York as they were hit with a $200,000 fine for a slew of violations, including unlicensed insurance activity.

Very few private citizens have cars that sit idle for days or weeks at a time, so the Turo marketplace is populated by cars that are solely used as rentals, much the same as the Airbnb properties which are occasionally purged from the system. There is a lack of due diligence from both parties in the transaction, since quite often neither one will be completely knowledgeable of their personal liability.

The service is open to abuse from car owners falsely claiming that renters have caused damage to the vehicle. Things get murkier still if a accident occurs and the renter blames a mechanical fault on the car. By simply being the 'platform' that connects the two parties, the company can easily distance itself from any kind of conflict resolution and customers making a complaint may have a hard time getting a reply via email, something easily ignored.

The notion of insurance is a big one for companies such as Turo and Airbnb, since they are asking people to put at risk perhaps the two most expensive possessions they own, their home and car. Both companies make bold reassurances about million-dollar insurance coverage, but as we've seen, Airbnb's is a last resort after you've maxed out your own coverage and Turo's may not be nearly enough. When they were still RelayRides, a renter was fatally injured in a collision which injured four other people. They sued the estate of the deceased driver, the owner of the car and RelayRides. The case was settled out of court so no information is available on the final figure but it is difficult to imagine it being covered by the $1m. State-by-state, Turo operates in a spectrum of gray areas, from probably maybe okay to nearly definitely shouldn't be doing this.

The ones who want to work for these companies at such cost to themselves should enjoy it while it lasts, however. The biggest burden for the tech companies are people, whether complaining about losing money by working for them or perhaps being classified as actual employees who need looking after, and the race is on to get rid of them altogether. The CEO of Uber, Travis Kalanick, has said that he looks forward to replacing the entire fleet with self-driving cars.

1.7 Conclusion

It is curious that the myth of the sharing economy pervades when there is so much evidence to show that it doesn't work. The more that unfortunately-named startups go on about rebuilding community and being agents for powerful change, the more false it feels. It is community according to their set of rules, at once an attempt to emulate an idealized version of how communities were historically supposed to act, and an ever-present corporate interest in the minutiae of daily interactions. The companies trying to get you to buy dinner from your neighbors, buy lifts from them, rent their power tools, act like pushy parents at a kids dance. Without them to force interactions between one another, we'll spend all our days stumbling around unaware of who we're living alongside. They want you to meet your neighbors, but want every meeting to be a transaction where they receive a bit of money.

All of the 'pay your neighbors to do stuff' companies operate because there are people, the service users, who value their time more highly in relation to their neighbors. Each task they pay for is in most cases something they are unwilling to do themselves, since in most cases it would be far more economical to learn a new skill than repeatedly pay someone else to perform it. It is not worth studying to become an electrician or plumber in order to be able to carry out the kind of repairs most homeowners are faced with. An individual could easily take several cooking lessons which would allow them to prepare their own meals rather than pay a neighbor to do it for them or continue buying takeaway food.

Communities either happen or they don't. Anyone who has lived in several areas will know that there were places where they had a much stronger relationship with their neighbors than in others. They don't need organizing in a formal sense and they certainly don't need to be monetized. It is perhaps due to young professionals' skewed world-views that so many companies are trying to sell the idea that we're all strangers and need to be forced to get to know one another.

Certainly young, predominantly single or childless people have less reason or chance to form bonds with those living around them. As soon as children appear it becomes practically unavoidable to form some level of acquaintance with people in the same situation living in the immediate area.

Although the on-demand economy companies have enjoyed huge benefits by catching governments and regulators unawares, a certain level of pushback has begun now that the dust has settled. In April 2016, Pennsylvania fined Uber $11.4m for operating without approval for 6 months in 2012. Although it was the highest fine handed down by the state's Public Utilities Commission, it was far less than the $50m suggested by judges the year before.

John McAfee, millionaire founder of the anti-virus software firm that bears his name, thinks that there is a war being fought against the 'gig economy'. He wrote in the International Business Times about the excessively-punitive regulations being introduced in Los Angeles to try and reign in people gaming the short term rental systems made possible by companies like Airbnb. He felt it excessive that the state was trying to limit people doing short-term rentals for only a...short term, in this case 90 days of the year. This limit would be more than enough for the kind of casual operators that are supposed to be Airbnb's primary source of accommodation. As various studies have shown, these people actually make up less than 20% of the userbase, with the rest of the stock coming from hardcore landlords who are doing it as a full-time endeavor. The new rules would also prevent people from renting out properties which weren't their primary residence, another issue that he took exception to.

2.1 Drinking the cool-aid: startup culture

The early days of home computing meant hours spent working through thick manuals and lots of trial and error. Looking back, it is amazing that the technology took off in such a way, given its nearly complete disregard for user experience. It relied on a core group of people who possessed the mindset to spend hundreds of hours hunched over their machines working out how to make them do their bidding. They were rewarded not only with machines that did what they promised, but also an intimate understanding of fundamental computer concepts. They had no choice but to become familiar with programming and the relationship between software and hardware. Any biography of a tech giant's founder will tell a common story of childhood years spent making their own games, programs or even hardware.

In the same way that early car owners had to essentially be mechanics, early computer users had to quickly become technology experts. Now cars are so complex that many repairs are not only out of reach of their owner, but also their local garage.

User experience is now the main priority when designing tech products. Anyone who has seen a small child or even infant using a tablet computer has marveled at how quickly they've picked it up. Really there is nothing for them to learn, the tablet computer works and reacts to their inquisitive fingers in the same way everything else in their world does. They touch what they are interested in and some sort of reaction occurs.

When my parents put our first PC in our home, my father was already in his 50s and lacked the patience or the time needed to learn how to make this expensive thing sitting on the desk work. Like many parents, however, he had realized or been convinced that it was very important that his family own one of these machines, despite the then-murky benefits. It has only been recently, specifically since he was able to buy a Kindle Fire tablet for about 70 times less than he paid for the PC, that he has begun using the Internet on a daily basis. As long as things 'just work' he has no need or desire to dig into the workings. In the developed world, his generation will probably be the last for which technology such as we use now will either be a wonderful new invention, an annoyance they can't fully understand or something of absolutely zero interest in their lives.

The globe-spanning tentacles of technology, which have spread with sometimes dizzying pace since the first home computers began occupying desk space some three decades ago, originate from a central location, a place which is often ground zero for the observable effects of online technology in the real world.

California is no stranger to being gently invaded by those lured by the promise of sudden wealth, unobtainable anywhere else. The tech boom has often been described as the second gold rush. Stories of incredible valuations and dramatic IPOs make many decide to try their luck. Of course, it wouldn't be a proper repeat of the past without a strong sense of 'this time it's different'. In a way it is; instead of blindly digging for gold guided by nothing more than rumor and intuition, people are making their own luck, reliant more on the strength of their ideas and more importantly, their ability to get others to buy into those ideas. Like the gold rush, however, many will ultimately leave no better off than when they arrived. Again, the only people actually getting rich may be those selling the pickaxes.

The catchall term for any of the large vehicles being used to ferry Silicon Valley employees to work every morning, the 'Google bus' has been one of the flashpoints of tension for the residents of San

Francisco who are not involved in the tech community. On the surface the buses are a sensible alternative to lots of workers taking their own cars, with the companies paying for them themselves. There have been a number of consequences to the scheme, however, which again illustrate the disconnect between both the companies and local government, and the companies and residents.

Until the beginning of 2014, the Google buses were operating completely illegally by using the city's municipal bus stops to pick up their passengers, an action which incurs a $271 fine. Users of city buses complained of congestion because of company buses using the stops. It was estimated that the tech companies collectively owed the city between $500m and $1bn in fines for this decade-long practice. No fines were ever issued, however; instead, after working with the companies flouting the law, the Municipal Transport Authority (MTA) announced that the various companies would now pay a $1 per time fee for using the city's stops.

This reduced Google's potential liability from over $27m each year (if they were made to start paying the fine) to $100,000, although it is very doubtful they would keep the buses running if they were forced to pay a fine each time. It was particularly galling for the residents who demanded action on this that Google was allowed to break the law for a decade with no punishment, then just be asked to pay a nominal charge from then on. In all other cases, the city is extremely diligent at issuing fines for this particular violation and plenty of private motorists are hit with the $271 charge if they are caught dropping someone off at a bus stop. The MTA has also been running a proof-of-payment enforcement scheme which involves checking people as they leave a city bus and giving them a $100 fine if they can't produce a ticket. This has been running since 2005 despite collecting far less for the city in fines than it costs to run the scheme.

Critics say that the city is focused on targeting and penalizing vulnerable working class people, while at the same time ignoring the tech companies who openly flout the law. Once the city gave its approval for using public bus stops, rents, property prices and evictions around the stops reportedly rose. The miles driven by employees in their own cars, which the tech companies want to cut, may be finding their way on to the roads anyway, as people on lower incomes are pushed out of the city because of a lack of affordable housing and will have to drive further into work each day.

As the number of startups continues to grow, along with the number of failures, more stories emerge about the kind of mismanagement that only seems to exist in these kind of companies, an adherence to quirk and kitsch over any other interior design style, prioritization of new age team-building techniques and willful disregard for established business practices. Underneath all this are more serious trends, ones that point to employees both being the victims of badly-run companies and sacrificed to ensure the financial benefit of others.

Inspired by the famously revolutionary workspaces of Google and Facebook, many startups seek to emulate their rule-breaking atmosphere but on a smaller scale. Often that means copying the worst elements of those methods and doing so purely for impact and bragging rights. For cash-strapped startups yet to turn a profit this is a curious extravagance. Beyond being just a job, the founders demand complete dedication from their staff which can mean more than just asking them to put in long hours. The way that some are run share similar methodology to the way cults operate. The staff are first enthused by being told that they are special and that being accepted into the company is an unparalleled achievement that separates them from everyone else. They are then informed of the nearly divine importance of the mission that they are working on, a mission that to do no less than something which is going to change the world as they know it. Members of the company will often use something akin to a private language, pointless terms that are not the usual corporate buzzwords, but local only to their organization.

The intentional lack of overt managerial structure promotes democracy and equality while nurturing a confusing, passive-aggressive environment which can leave staff open to discrimination, sexism and seemingly arbitrary decisions that come out of nowhere. The employees are kept going through the months and years of punishing schedules by the promise of a fat reward at the end when the company goes public. They may have accepted lower wages in return for stock options, although these may also have come with strings attached.

At the top of the startup foodchain are the venture capitalists. They are the ones signing the checks and deciding which ideas are going to get a shot at success. They get the best stock options. Next are the executives, the creators of the site or service, they are most likely on the same equity terms as the VCs. At the bottom are the ground troops, full-time employees who have been hired as part of the rapid expansion made possible by the influx of investor money. They can forgo a high salary in exchange for more stock options with the company and the promise of a big pay out come initial public offering day. The catch for this group is that they are often subject to a 'lock-in' clause, preventing them from selling their stock in the company until a set time after the IPO.

The early investors get preferential treatment regarding the stock, since they are allowed to sell before the company goes public. This can net a huge profit for them as typically in the run up to an IPO, excitement is building that the general investing public is going to get a chance to own part of this exciting and fabulous new company and everyone is positive that the price is going to go through the roof. Early investors can therefore sell their stock to those who weren't aware of the company in its early days but now wish to get onboard.

Late investors can get an agreement promising them a minimum value for their shares, even if the public price falls through the floor when it hits the stock market. If this happens, the investors will get more shares to bring their total up to the agreed upon minimum. This in turn means the shares of the people still locked into owning them decrease further. The more rounds of funding the startup goes through, the more shares are issued and the more each employee's equity holding gets diluted.

Often, employees are seduced by the very notion of owning lots of shares in a company, and are ignorant both of the terms and of their stake's true value. Depending on how the wind is blowing at the time, the heads of the company may even change their minds and decide against an IPO, rendering options utterly worthless.

The most painful recent example of the disadvantage employees are at when it comes to the big payday concerns the company Good Technology, once a member of the unicorn club, now the subject of a lawsuit brought by former employees.

Good Technology was in actuality the last incarnation of a company called SpringThings which began life in 2000. 9 years later it became (after a series of transitions) Good Technology, a company which let enterprises manage employees' company-issued mobile devices. Shortly before the planned IPO, a reassessment of the landscape made the executives and investors back off from going public. Several tech companies had just taken the leap and most were under-performing, and the company began looking for a buyer. Believing that they were still worth $1bn, they rejected an offer of $825m before finally accepting $425m from Blackberry.

This sale price put employees' common stock at $0.44 a share, slightly down from the $4.32 it had been a year earlier. Worse still, the employees were taxed on the perceived value of the shares before it was suddenly sold to Blackberry. Some employees' tax bills were so high that they had to use their savings or even borrow money to be able to pay.

The employee's lawsuit alleges that the company's CEO, Christy Wyatt, accepted the Blackberry deal because of a large retention plan bonus which her and her executive team would get for staying with the company until the deal was completed. It is also claimed that 6 of the 9 members of the company's board of directors were either founders or managing directors of the venture capital firms which invested in the company in the first place. After the sale, Christy Wyatt walked away with nearly $6m, and in total the VC firms got over $160m. Some of the employees ended up paying more in taxes than they earned in salary. Quite often, the employees' first knowledge that something monumental has happened to their company is when it actually happens, like when they get to the office one morning and it is announced that the company has been sold and the doors are all locked.

The 400 employees at Zirtual, a four-year-old virtual assistant matchmaker, received an email one afternoon in August 2015 telling them that, effective immediately, the company was ceasing operations and they were all out of a job. The founder, Maren Kate Donovan, was able to sell the company and the employees were offered the chance to reapply for their old jobs but this time as independent contractors, not full-time employees. The month before this rather drastic action, Maren Kate Donovan appeared in Fortune magazine, where she said:

'And be transparent. Employees who can trust in the company and its management are much more likely to stay committed to the mission.'

That there are so many companies of staggering size concentrated in one area means that dramatic change is inevitable. San Francisco's situation is also unique in that the jobs created there are not intended for the residents. The majority of people who seek employment at a tech company will have relocated to live there and many are single. This has caused high prices and short supply in the rental market. The gap in wages between those in the tech sector and those not is large and growing. So not only is accommodation getting more expensive, but so too things such as groceries, restaurants and services. Small business owners who know there are thousands of employees on six-figure salaries would be stupid to not raise their prices.

Given how the Internet has changed the landscape of employment and made the world a smaller space, it is perhaps strange that so many of these companies congregate in one area. If they were to be spread around the country then it would be much more beneficial, since the disposable income spent by the employees would be distributed to many more restaurants, cafes and shops. Also, the employees' need for housing would have less of an impact on the market as a whole, still increasing prices but not nearly at the rate that San Francisco has seen.

America has or has had huge automotive and aerospace industries. General Motors has production facilities in 8 states, and between them the major Japanese car manufacturers cover another 7, all spread out amongst the central and eastern states. They are more often than not welcomed to an area because they are huge employers of local people. Jobs created due to the tech economy which local people can take advantage of are in areas which service the requirements of the tech workers. Tesla, which wants to be to cars what Apple is to computers, has one factory, in California.

2.2 House of (business) cards: tech lobbying

Practically all traditional businesses selling products or services have suffered in some way over the last 20 years. The slow ones have died, the quick ones adapted. Some of the biggest have been able to weather things to a certain extent and spend their time trying to play catchup and bemoaning the sudden rise of the successors. There is little sympathy for the bricks-and-mortar establishments which have failed to move with the times. While people may talk nostalgically of the way that high streets and town centers used to be, they are driven by pragmatism to shop online like everyone else. It is easier and cheaper to buy things over the Internet. Many of the people who do make the journey to traditional stores are often only there to do the one thing they can't on an online shop, handle the products; once satisfied, they can go home and get it from Amazon. If they live in a major metropolitan area such as London, they can have it delivered within an hour.

In 2014, Amazon paid the British government £2.4m in taxes. The same year, it was given £2.5m from the Scottish government to help build a new distribution center in Dunfermline. Their earnings that year amounted to $4.2bn globally (£147m in the UK). Facebook famously paid £4,327 corporation tax in the UK in 2014. After an extremely negative reaction from the press and public they announced in February 2016 that they would overhaul their tax operations. Instead of funneling all their revenue through their Ireland office, the revenue they make from their biggest advertisers would remain in the UK and therefore be taxable. However, from years of reporting net losses in the UK, the company has built up deferred tax assets worth £21m. They can offset this amount against future tax bills.

The large advertisers spending their money with Facebook require dedicated staff in the UK to deal with their accounts, and this is the source of the money that Facebook said will remain in the UK.

Advertising for smaller business is done automatically and the proceeds from this group will be moved to Ireland, where the corporation tax rate is only 12.5%. However, it has been claimed that the big-ticket advertisers make up only a fifth of Facebook's total advertising income, estimated to have been nearly $800m in 2015. Current tax rules in the UK do not tax the profits made by companies on sales of products and services made outside the UK, instead, the tax is charged based on what part of a company's profits were generated by the offices they run in the UK. This means that come tax time, the UK branch of whatever tech company can find their importance to the company downplayed quite dramatically.

In order to reduce their tax liability that year, Facebook gave £35m to their staff in stock bonuses, resulting in an accounting loss of £28.5m for the year.

The offices of the large tech companies are not integrated into society in the same way that traditional businesses are, even large nationwide chains. The biggest supermarket chains, for example, have locations throughout the country. They employ local people in each place and understand the importance of being seen to support local causes. They are frequently accused of being behind the death of the UK high streets by taking shoppers to big retail parks outside of town but at the very least they are employers and pay taxes and the areas around the stores often attract other businesses. Facebook has a single office in the UK; it doesn't care where its employees are from. They are people who have spent years learning a very specialized set of technical skills. They are willing and able to pay a high price for good accommodation in the city, which raises prices at a much faster rate than in other areas. Facebook's 830 UK staff handled £105m in 2014 versus the 220,000 people who work for Tesco, which generated £2bn in profits in the same year.

The former chief economist of the World Bank, Nobel Prize winning Josef Stiglitz, declared Apple's tax setup 'fraud', rightly questioning how the biggest company in the world can attribute the lion's share of its earnings to a few hundred employees working out of Ireland. Independent assessments of the company's tax liability if its current arrangement is declared illegal put the figure at around $8bn. In their defense, Apple has stated that it too wishes for an overhaul of the US corporate tax system which would allow it to repatriate its earnings at a fair rate.

This type of tax battle is nothing new. Opponents complain about the companies dodging tax and exploiting loopholes. The companies reply that they pay every penny that they are legally required to. The government tries to keep attention away from questions about why the loopholes and tax havens can't be closed down since their biggest and most influential backers are using the same services to squirrel away their earnings. In the UK at least, getting tough with tech companies which don't necessarily even need to be there can be difficult for government, especially when they are championing the creation of East London's Tech City, a rather less cutesy-sounding name than Silicon Roundabout, which it was previously.

A group of tech companies, including the big names like Apple, Google and Amazon have come together to form a lobbying group. Known as 'Financial Innovation Now', it seeks to achieve favorable policies which will make things easier for fintech (financial technology) startups, and also naturally the established companies. Fintech startups are concentrating on things like real-time payments and lending to both consumers and small businesses.

In late 2015, an investigation by the Guardian newspaper shed light on the scale of Google's lobbying efforts on and the effect that they have had not only in America, but also in the EU. It has been claimed that the company spent more money on political lobbying than any other since 2012. The Obama administration's chief technology officer is an ex-Google employee, along with several others. In the 2016 election cycle, the company has made donations of between $1,000 and $10,000 to 162 members of congress, both Democrat and Republican.

Aggressive lobbying by big business is often mistakenly thought of as a purely American issue, yet another factor which makes up their famously inefficient government. When the proposal was before the EU that perhaps Google should be broken up into smaller companies, Members of the European Parliament (MEPs) received letters, in many cases identical ones, from the US members of Congress who benefited from Google campaign donations, asking them to oppose this proposal in the interest of free markets. The EU isn't nearly as enamored with Google as the Obama administration. It has launched two antitrust investigations into the company.

On the surface, the complaints closely mirror those that were levied against Microsoft during its famous court battle in the mid-90s. Then the company was accused of creating unfair advantage by bundling its Internet Explorer browser with the Windows operating system. Now, the EU is questioning whether Google is doing the same by forcing any handset maker wishing to use the Android operating system to include the Google Search and Chrome browser apps. While the Android operating system is free for any manufacturer to use and adapt as they see fit, if manufacturers want consumers to be allowed to access the full suite of Google software, then they have to agree not to install one of the modified versions of the operating system, or their own versions of Google's apps. The willingness of the EU to go after Google has raised uncomfortable comparisons with the decision by the FTC not to pursue any action of its own.

Google's efforts to reshape the legislative landscape to its own advantage are much more sophisticated than simply paying lobbying firms millions of dollars for them to bother politicians. The company has a multi-pronged strategy of both overt and extremely subversive programs. At its most direct, it meant co-founder Larry Page meeting directly with the then-Commission president, José Manuel Barroso, at the company's Mountain View headquarters. Despite specifically being asked not to discuss the ongoing antitrust investigation, it was talked about for an hour during the visit. Closer to the deadline, CEO Eric Schmidt became involved, also contacting Barroso directly. Ultimately the Commission didn't side with Google and reopened the investigation, rather than accept any of the settlements proposed by Google.

At the other end of the scale is where the long-game money goes. Google donates heavily to both academic institutions and think-tanks. Quite often, they are then the subject of studies run by these places which seem to favorably support the notion that Google is doing no wrong in the world. George Mason University's Law and Economics Center received a total of $762,000 up to the end of 2013 from the company. They have published numerous studies which support Google's claims that they have not violated any laws.

By getting in on the ground floor, by buying favorable influence at high ranking educational institutions, the company is aiming to softly mould the opinions of those people who are likely to themselves be in positions of power and influence in the future. The opinion of academics and experts is often deferred to when it comes to complex technical matters, yet it is rarely asked if perhaps the experts whose views can be so influential are not just another type of lobbyist, incapable of delivering an honest assessment of the company due to the amount of donations involved. This is best exemplified by Professor Joshua Wright, who published several Google funded studies of the company while at George Mason. He later went on to become an FTC commissioner. This, however, was a step too far for most and he quickly promised to stay out of any of the FTC's dealings with Google for two years after his appointment.

Google doesn't know where the students and staff will ultimately end up years down the line. There is a high probability, however, that some will eventually end up working for a government body which may one day turn its attentions to Google. The company must be very happy when it loses high-ranking employees to government positions, and those who have spent years in academia, looking at data which seems to support all the claims that the company makes, can go out in to the world as kind of nerdy sleeper cells, ready to be activated should the company ever need a ruling to go its own way.

By default, people are inclined to believe or at least place some stock in the findings published by academic institutions, unless it's a report by Snickers University debunking the link between sugar and diabetes. When it comes to credible establishments then it can be difficult for the casual reader to keep in mind that the figures supporting the findings may have been massaged in some way, and figures can always be pushed and pulled in different directions to achieve a desired result.

That Google provides services which rely on their own visibility in search rankings creates a situation rife with the possibility of monopolization. How can other providers of map websites or video websites ever be confident that despite their best efforts, Google Maps and YouTube won't always appear at the top, even if perhaps they are not strictly the most relevant result for the person submitting the query?

It isn't difficult to recognize the pattern of behavior here. In the same way that sharing economy startups happily ignored laws and regulations under the guise of innovation, so to are the fintech startups beginning to claim that they shouldn't be regulated in the same way as the established players because they operate in a fundamentally different way. Coming, as we are, out of one of the biggest financial depressions in recent memory, it seems very dangerous to allow the same kind of people with the same kind of thinking to start lending to consumers and handling things like mortgages and insurance.

The creation of Financial Innovation Now was seen by some as a reaction to a banking industry whitepaper published by The Clearing House, an association of 24 large banks. The paper argued that there is an un-level playing field between the traditional financial institutions and the new wave of small startups.

The next generation of fintech companies are going to be able to leverage the huge amount of bad feeling that the public currently has towards traditional banking institutions. Bad banking and lending practices were blamed for the financial crash of 2008 so the timing could not be more fortuitous for nimble young companies to rush in and proclaim how different they are. Like most other startups discussed already, they will no doubt use works like 'sharing' 'community' and 'disrupt' while avoiding terms like 'unregulated' and 'illegal'.

2.3 Better together: lending to strangers

Starting around 2010, the UK saw a sudden influx of what were called 'payday lenders', companies who offered quick loans for small amounts that were designed to be repaid when the borrower received their next paycheck. They quickly became notorious for the high annual interest they charged, in some cases up to 3000%. The lenders claimed that the loans were never intended to be held for such a long time, but many people found themselves trapped in an ever-deepening hole of debt when they were unable to pay off the loan in a timely manner.

Loans of two or three hundred pounds would quickly multiply to many thousands. There was more than one reported case of suicide caused by the stress of being continually hounded for money. These companies specifically targeted vulnerable people whose income sometimes wasn't enough to cover all their monthly expenses. The government stepped in and quickly pushed through new legislation to protect consumers. In some instances, thousands of borrowers had their loans entirely written off.

These companies were rather inelegant operations. All they needed was a stupid but catchy name, an easy to use website and a TV advert. There was no hint of social mission or advanced technology underpinning what they were doing. New lenders have wised up; instead of marketing themselves as intentionally flippant, they are going the opposite way, trumpeting the way that they can use data about potential borrowers to make smart lending decisions.

Like every other area of business where its possible to squeeze in yet another cheery looking startup, the finance industry is awash with fintech companies looking to disrupt banks' businesses. Some companies, such as Upstart, are trying to build a bigger picture of a potential borrower's financial health by looking at not only their credit score, but also their education and job prospects. By offering lower rates to those with the brightest futures they are obviously targeting the high end of the market, populated by extremely low-risk customers.

What these customers all have in common is choice. Most of the other startups see more opportunity in lending to people at the other end of the scale, people with no choice who have been refused loans by traditional institutions.

The startups claim they are offering a service to a large group of people criminally underrepresented by loan providers. Critics see predatory lenders targeting people who may have been refused loans in the past for good reason.

Investment in fintech startups has climbed from $1.8bn in 2010 to $19bn in 2015. Anthony Jenkins, the chief executive of Barclays, said that the industry is facing a series of Uber moments. Jobs in the banking industry are expected to fall by around 30% over the next 10 years. Not all of these job losses are being blamed on startups; new regulations brought in as a result of the financial crisis are also playing a part.

The current test-bed for new ways for consumers to carry out financial transactions is in China; startups there have quickly reached prominence because they often have extremely large and powerful parent companies backing them. Alipay, obviously backed by Alibaba, handled over three times the amount of payments that PayPal did in 2015. China has already passed the 'tipping point' where fintech companies now have similar numbers of users as traditional banks.

Unlike the taxi industry, which was practically uniformly against Uber from day one, those in the banking sector do not all share the same opinion when it comes to newcomers. Banks have been generally keen to embrace new technologies and most if not all high street banks offer free online banking as standard. In fact, the vast majority of customers' interactions with their banks are now online. So currently they are split between those who see this as a next logical step and those who perhaps have seen the effect startups have wrought in other sectors and are afraid for their own jobs.

With a lack of regulation comes a lack of protection for the customer. Unregulated companies don't have to go to the same lengths to ensure that customers can repay their loans before issuing them, nor are they required to reimburse customers who have had money taken out of their account without their authorization. Regulated or not, there wouldn't be many startups who would be happy to lend to extremely risky borrowers; not carrying out the necessary checks would only hurt them in the long run if they were lending their own money. Thankfully for them, there is a way around this.

Startups love having the public do the work for them, more often than not without what would be considered fair remuneration. Uber wants you to use your own car and pay for your own petrol, Taskrabbit wants you to use your own everything. In the sharing economy, all the risk is offloaded onto the service provider, not the company doing the matchmaking. Interestingly, despite its relative infancy, peer-to-peer lending has already matured along much the same lines as services such as Airbnb. Originally, there were a large amount of small lenders lending directly to borrowers. Now, in the same way that most of Airbnb's profits come from a tiny pool of super-landlords, the P2P system has become dominated by large institutional investors, for example hedge funds. This has led to attempts to rebrand P2P as 'marketplace lending'.

The friendly face and approachability of these new P2P lending platforms poses a danger to borrowers in that, psychologically, they may not treat the transaction with the same amount of seriousness as they would a loan from a traditional institution. Defaulting on P2P carries the same negative impact on their credit score as defaulting on any other kind of loan. Whereas currently the majority of loans issued are for refinancing purposes, there is a push into the area of new financing. Startups offering money for things such as weddings, tuition and elective medical procedures have sprung up to try and reroute borrowing that has typically been done on credit cards.

Sites such as Prosper.com use a mix of verified and unverified data. The unverified data is the personal photos the borrower uploads along with the story of why they want a loan and what it will be used for. Studies have shown that lenders are reasonably adept at judging the credit-worthiness of a person based on a mixture of these two information types. On the other side, the system also highlights people's inherent biases, with attractive women benefiting from lower-interest loans and non-white borrowers paying significantly higher interest than white borrowers in similar financial categories.

The two biggest P2P sites, Prosper and Lendingclub, were both required to seek approval from the Securities and Exchange Commission. Unusually for an Internet startup, both quietly complied. Of course, it is a lot less of a burden to comply with SECC rules than it is to suddenly make tens of thousands of people officially classed as employees. Despite this official seal of approval, lenders would get nothing back if the sites were to suddenly go belly-up.

Some lenders have discovered an unexpected problem while trying to give away money: a lack of borrowers. Like all startups, the fintech companies are primarily concerned with growth, or at least the appearance of growth. There is currently a much greater number of lenders than borrowers. To try and rectify this, companies are looking for ways to get people to borrow money that they might not otherwise want. Instead of waiting for the customer to come to them cap in hand, they are going out and putting the caps in people's hands themselves. Prosper, a San Francisco-based market lender, partnered with Spirit Airlines to offer loans to people to get them on holiday. Prosper also owns a company which enables medical clinics to offer loans to people who want elective surgical procedures. Lending Club has similar setups in place.

As many others do, the fintech startups like to wrap themselves in the warm, comforting blanket that is the term 'social'. In this case it's people like you and me lending to people like you and me. Lending Club allows investors to pool their resources, so you don't need to loan someone the full $10,000 they want, you can just fund part of it. In actuality, the amount of aww-shucks people lending a helping hand to their fellow man is very low; the social lending sites are primarily the preserve of massive institutional investors. Santander, after breaking up with Uber, decided to stop feeling sorry for itself and get back into the game when it signed an agreement with Lending Club to purchase a fixed portion ($30m or 50%, whichever was less) of their business each month. In January 2016, however, it announced that its heart had been broken too many times and that it had $1bn worth of consumer debt for sale, having lost $123m in defaults on unsecured loans. Not long after J.P.Morgan Chase took the debt off Santander's hands.

When P2P lending first began, borrowers wrote a little story to go along with their pitch and were encouraged to add photos to make it more personal. Now that the large investor firms have moved in, the majority of loan requests made on the site are approved within 10 seconds. By 2014, 65% of loans were snapped up whole, instead of being funded fractionally by a group of individuals. In July 2016 this practice led to the resignation of the CEO of Lending Club after an investigation in to the sale of $22m worth of loans to a single investor.

A major obstacle to success for these types of companies comes again in the need for growth. A large proportion of the borrowers who use the platform are unlikely to do so repeatedly. To ensure a steady influx of new customers, they may have to gradually reduce how stringent they are in weeding out potential bad borrowers. Because of the relative youth of all P2P companies - even the oldest has only been around since 2005 - they are able to brag about low default rates simply because many of their customers haven't been customers long enough to risk defaulting.

The notion of P2P lending isn't a bad one in itself. It doesn't affect people not using the service in any way and, as long as investors are made aware of the potential risks, then they can enjoy a potentially healthy return on their money. People lending to people was always going to be strictly small-time, however, and the social platforms must have realized this when they began. There is a limited amount of people with spare capital to invest in this manner, a smaller proportion still who would feel comfortable lending it to essentially a complete stranger. Once they have chosen someone looking to borrow money, it may be several years before it is completely repaid so unless they have a very large amount of initial funds, they may not put more money into a site for a long time.

In hindsight it seems inevitable now that the big players would come in and buy up all the debt as soon as the borrowers were making their applications. The problem with this closely mirrors one of the reasons the subprime mortgage industry was such a con: these consumer debts can be bought by one entity, bundled, repackaged and sold to another interested party. Each time the debt is sold on, it becomes more difficult to clearly see exactly where it originated, and how the debt is graded can also be altered as it changes hands. It may contain a toxic mix of good and bad loans, the bad ones with almost no chance of being paid off. By the time these securities come out of the other end, they may be purchased either by individual investors or investment funds. At some point someone is left holding the bag when the original borrowers suddenly start to default on the loans en masse. More big firms buying up more debt no questions asked creates more P2P startups who must accept more risk in order to find more customers. The risk to consumers is the one that always faces people who choose to refinance: they may start spending again and end up with the refinanced debt and also a brand new debt.

Although the amounts they are moving are still only a fraction of what the banks handle, the P2P companies have still set up billions of dollars' worth of loans between them. Given what has (or hasn't) been learned since the financial crisis, it seems risky to say the least to have so many unsecured loans made to people who have obviously struggled to find approval elsewhere, made by private lenders who may not have the spare resources available to absorb a large loss if things go wrong.

The buzzwords floating around like 'social', 'community' and 'responsible' reveal more than just wishful thinking or outright lying on the part of the startup founder. There is a historical difference of opinion in the realm of finance over the very concept of something being socially beneficial and the value thinking such as this has. It is perhaps no less relevant now at a time when we are being encouraged to lend to our neighbors (through a middleman).

Nobel Prize-winning economist Friedrich von Hayek had some strong thoughts on the word social, and its use as an adjective. He said the word social was a 'weasel word' which destroyed the meaning of whatever it was attached to. Milton Friedman, who won the prize two years after von Hayek, was similarly against the notion of social justice in the financial markets.

In 2009, the then-chairman of the Financial Services Authority, Lord Adair Turner, caused an outcry from the financial sector by going against the views of Friedman and von Hayek. While he maintained that the notion of social justice in finance was a lie, Lord Turner argued that the financial sector had grown too large and that a great deal of the products they were offering were of no social value whatsoever and should be done away with.

He pinned the blame for our monetary woes on the sheer complexity of the financial products on offer, products which were sometimes not fully understood even by the people who spent their days trading in them.

Due to the nature of the product, there is a definite limitation on the amount of business that P2P lenders can do. They will have to either expand outwards into new markets, or tunnel downwards, taking on riskier and riskier borrowers. Of course, the actual risk is taken on by the lenders, not the companies. Regardless of how successful they are, at some point growth will grind to a halt. It is at this point that we can expect them to start exploring other financial products.

Several startups already exist which are trying to make the trading of shares as easy as buying music from iTunes. So why not push the boat out and get us all involved in trading derivatives, credit default swaps and pork futures? The companies who will end up marketing this capability in a brightly colored app, a stupid name and a few million dollars of VC funds again won't be shouldering any risk from the wild transactions that the general public will suddenly be able to make. They'll just take a commission and several steps back.

Again, we can look to China for a glimpse at not only a possible future, but one pushed well past the point of absurdity. For the majority of people in the West, stock information is something that floats across the bottom of the news channel, a meaningless mess of symbols and numbers. In China, however, the stock market is something of a national obsession, with over 90 million active private investors. In 2015 we got a glimpse into this world when the media started showing footage from inside the public rooms of the brokerage houses, where citizens sat watching the figures going up and down all day. Some did knitting while they watched, some read. Tips and rumours are excitedly traded online and on the street corner. That year was a rollercoaster for the Chinese market as it climbed 200%, then lost a third of its value in a month before rebounding again. The beginning of 2016 saw a disastrous effort to control the market through the use of a cut-off switch which automatically halted trading if prices dropped too much.

The Chinese have fewer places to invest their money, which may account for the popularity of trading stocks. The British are as a whole a more cautious bunch and seem happy with government-backed ISAs which keep the taxman away from their savings. There are growing numbers of amateur traders, although as of now they are a private bunch who trade from home and don't discuss it much.

Most heads of technology companies may agree with the thinking of von Hayek and Friedman, that financial products were neither just nor unjust and could be removed from the field of human ethics. This sounds very much like the kind of description often applied to the Internet and computers as a whole.

As the number of fintech companies offering loans increases, there will be more people fighting over a finite amount of customers. In order to keep growing, the only way they can go is down, since people with good credit scores both have less need for loans and are easily able to get them from traditional lenders, so why take the risk on an unproven startup? In 2013 Lending Club slightly relaxed the minimum credit score that it required from potential borrowers. To help get rid of the nasty taste that subprime left in everyone's mouth, these high risk loans are now being described as 'near prime' and the charmingly hopeful 'emerging prime'. Given the short amount of time these companies have been operating, it remains to be seen if they are able to weather the storm of a sudden spike in defaults.

We've seen that many of today's exciting new services are just old-fashioned ways of doing things, but repackaged. In small communities long ago, there would have been someone good at building, someone good at mending, someone good at baking. They would have supported one another and exchanged services. Then money and streaming video came along and we were able to stop pretending that we enjoyed spending time with our neighbors. The latest digital endeavor to hearken back to a simpler time is the concept of P2P insurance, which are just mutuals in disguise. The concept is that a group of like-minded people (often called friends on the service websites) band together and pay money into a common pot. If a claim is made by one of the members then it is paid out; at the end of the year, whatever money is left is divided back up and paid back. By grouping together, the friends can obtain a better rate from the insurance company than if they were to approach it individually. It is the latest thing to use the word 'disrupt'.

The first and most immediate problem with this is the loss of anonymity suffered by all members of the group, the second is the potential pressure faced when considering making a claim, knowing that it will directly decrease the amount of money that everyone else gets back at the end of the year.

If you are in a group of friends in same sense as Facebook friends, i.e. total strangers you have no feelings for, then this may not be an issue, but if they are actual real life friends then they may wonder if you really had to get that dent on your car fixed and perhaps you should have driven more carefully.

All these services aim to connect groups of people in similar circumstances or with similar values. They would be unlikely to group a very young driver with someone who has driven for 30 years without a claim. Friends are able to group together themselves without taking on anyone unknown to them. While mutual insurance offers many benefits, in some circumstances it may be dramatically less beneficial to be part of a pool, depending on the nature of the thing being insured and how the members are distributed.

It would be extremely risky for example for a group of people living in close proximity to buy home or car insurance together. If they were to be victims of a sudden weather event then they stand a real chance of all being affected at the same time. Having to also concern themselves with their friends' claims while sorting out their own and thinking about the dwindling pot would compound the stress of the situation and almost certainly cause an extreme amount of friction within the group.

This pot that the members create from their individual contributions is really just the deductible, or excess in the UK. These P2P services are another layer of middlemen which are essentially offering insurance on the deductible. A big claim would go straight to the insurance company as normal but the little things are designed to be covered by the pot. Normally, if something small goes wrong, then a person has a straight choice to make: do they pay to have the thing fixed or not? Having money in a P2P pot complicates this by turning the decision into 'what will they all think about me if I pay to have this fixed? We're only two months from the end of the year, they'll all think I'm selfish if I dip-in to the pot, nobody else has touched it all year...' If the people are indeed friends in real life, then claimants may find themselves having to justify their decision to take money out of the pot.

Quite likely, people using a P2P insurer will join a group of strangers who have shared interests. It would be difficult to get a sufficiently large group of friends or family together and convince each one to break their current insurance contract and band together. The P2P insurance model strongly promotes the idea of a moral contingent being integral to the success of the scheme, by which they mean guilt. For the group to walk away at the end of the year with the amazingly low premium they were promised when they signed up, everyone has to feel too guilty to make a claim, so the concept of the insurance becomes meaningless, since all members have done is go through this service (which gets a commission) and purposely left the money sitting there not doing anything when it may have been needed.

Again, the startups live in the world where we are all best friends because of the magic of Facebook. Few things bring out the selfishness in a person faster than personal injury or tragedy. Imaginary connections with people you have never met and will never meet don't count for much when a person is reeling after an accident. If social startups failed to get people to lend power tools to one another, will they be able to get them to insure together?

The subprime mortgage industry, commonly agreed to be the main factor in the most recent financial crisis, seemingly hasn't tarnished the word 'subprime' beyond salvage. Two other major subprime markets exist, one for credit cards and the other, which is much larger, for cars. A huge and profitable market has been growing at an impressive pace over the last 30 years and is only getting bigger.
It specializes in selling cars on finance deals to people who would otherwise find purchasing a car difficult or impossible due to their credit history. The customer can indeed get a car but the finance package will be at significantly higher interest than a normal dealer charges. Add in grossly marked-up extras and drivers can easy end up paying nearly twice the price of the car.

One of the biggest players in the subprime car market is Santander, who partnered with Uber in 2013 to offer leasing on cars so that people could get on the road and start being Uber drivers. The deal was abruptly ceased two years later without any explanation. It may have simply been a step too far for the company to be associated with the word 'subprime'. By this point, the public was far more knowledgeable about the dangers of extending credit to people who shouldn't really qualify so it was seen as a cynical move by Uber to push people towards this kind of finance deal.

The scheme was attractive to Uber for two reasons. Firstly they can never, ever have enough drivers; they aren't required to give any one driver a minimum amount of work and it is far more important to them that the customer isn't kept waiting too long, so the more cars on the road the better, even if it means each person earning less as a result. Secondly, the finance terms for the vehicles stipulated that it could only be used as an Uber car (keeping in mind that they aren't a taxi company); it could not be used for private use or for accepting fares for any other ride-hailing company. This was an excellent way to lock drivers in to using the Uber platform, something that they weren't legally allowed to do otherwise. So instead of paying drivers sign-up bonuses to keep them onboard, they could just ensure that the car couldn't be used for any other purpose. Several people were quick to fully break down the maths of the deals and posted warnings about how bad they were.

Since the payments for the car would be automatically deducted from the driver's Uber earnings and there was a mileage limit on the car, in some cases it was actually impossible to make the payments, meaning that drivers could be essentially working for free, since they couldn't make enough in fares to cover the cost of the car they could use for no other purpose than for going out and getting fares.

In November 2015 Uber announced that instead of pushing lucky drivers to Santander to sell their souls, they would offer the service themselves. A new subsidiary called Xchange Leasing was launched offering a slightly improved version of the old deal. Drivers could still expect to pay double the monthly costs that they would if they went to a regular dealership but they could break the lease for a $250 fine. The finance provider for Xchange Leasing is a company called Westlake Financial, recipient of $44m worth of fines from the Consumer Financial Protection Bureau for a raft of illegal practices.

Uber holds all the cards when it comes to the paying of the loan. Since drivers can only use the vehicle to work for Uber, they must either continue working for them and remain vulnerable to any of the sudden pay changes that Uber likes to make, or they can leave the car sitting outside their home and get another job to pay for it, not forgetting that they'll have to find some other way to get to their new workplace (how about hailing an Uber?) as they can't use their own car.

By their very nature, people in the subprime bracket are highly likely to eventually default on their loans. It seems that Uber is having to go after less and less desirable people to maintain their perceived growth rate. The company continually loses a large amount of drivers so the pressure is on to keep new signups coming in. The leasing program puts drivers effectively in bond, since they can't just delete the app and decide that they don't want to do it anymore. Drivers burdened with 20% or higher APR finance deals will more likely run themselves ragged trying to make the weekly payments for a longer period of time before eventually giving up and paying the $250 fine to break the contract, leaving them with a similarly broken credit rating.

The financial crisis was partly the result of lenders giving mortgages to people who shouldn't have been approved for them. When these people started to default on their mortgages, it had a catastrophic knock-on effect on the rest of the market. The new fintech startups will seek to differentiate themselves from traditional lenders in some way. They can probably make it easier and more convenient for apply for a loan. They will, however, be slaves to exactly the same thing as every other startup backed with lots of VC money: growth. Very quickly they will have to demonstrate rapid growth in order to justify the large valuations that have been placed on them.

The only way to grow quickly is to lend to more people. As soon as growth is prioritized over other things, there is a real, practically unavoidable risk that they will start lending to people who would otherwise be turned down for loans.

Sadly, it looks as though the same sequence of events which befell the taxi industry will be played out again in the financial sector. A new operator will open fast and wide, flush with VC capital. It will start lending to people at seemingly far superior rates than traditional lenders can match. It will all be done in minutes through an app. Banks will complain, the startup will say they aren't a financial business, just a tech one matching people who need money with people lending it. Government will accept the lie that they are different from any other kind of broker. In the strongest case, insignificant fines will be handed out; more likely, legislation will be amended to allow the startups to continue operating. When the stories of upset consumers start coming in, instead of just having a cleaner who didn't do a good job or an Uber driver who leered at you, this time it will involve people's homes and life savings.

2.4 Paperless, branchless: migration to online-only

Over the last few years, the UK government has been pushing to provide more and more public services online, principally as a way of cutting costs. The Digital by Default initiative aims to make administering personal services online the primary approach. For the majority of people, this is generally a much faster and more convenient way to do things such as pay for car tax, register to vote or renew a passport. Widely-quoted figures in the press talked of savings in the range of 10 to 50 times the cost of doing things over the telephone, by post or face-to-face. It is important to remember that the savings are savings for the government, not for individuals. Citizens are now burdened with the cost of obtaining the necessary computer equipment and paying the ongoing fee in order to access the Internet, not to mention the cost of time spent learning how to use everything.

The issue of the closure of offices which provide public services is a chicken and egg scenario. Places like banks point to both increased use of online services and decreased use of high street branches. With UK bank closures averaging 12 a week, many customers may be forced online rather than travel great distances or wait for the once-a-week mobile bank to trundle through town. 15 passport offices in the UK have been earmarked for closure, starting in March 2016.

Citizens Advice, formerly known as the Citizens Advice Bureau, is a UK charity which helps people with things such a housing, employment, tax, money and benefit problems. It has suffered massive cutbacks and closures across the country in the last few years as local councils slash budgets for services such as these. Despite the proliferation of up to date information online, this will negatively impact nearly all the citizens who would normally be in most need of help or assistance from the large number of staff and volunteers who run the organization.

40% of the British population will use the service at some point in their lives. It operates a well-designed website that was used by one third of the population in 2013. However accessible and easy on the eye a website may be, it will never replicate what a physical location can. The problems that people bring to Citizens Advice can be complicated and interconnected, not something that is easily typed into a search box. That a great many problems can also be straightforward and easily answered on the other hand may have encouraged local councils to think that the bricks-and-mortar locations were inefficient relics of the pre gov.uk website age.

Again this creates a large number of people who may now not have anywhere to talk with someone face-to-face about their problems, who may also lack the money and knowhow to buy and install the necessary IT equipment and who may be left with more questions than answers if they are unable to navigate the labyrinth of information available online regarding all aspects of public services. Citizens Advice saw a large increase in the number of people seeking debt advice as a result of the financial crisis, however they themselves seem to have fallen victim to the same thing due to cutbacks. Whether it be any one of the reasons mentioned, financial or lack of knowledge, a bare minimum of staffed locations should be kept for people who can't, or just don't want to use the online replacement.

When the UK's high street banks seriously began their program of branch closures, there was an idea kicked around briefly that they might work together in some areas by residing in a single larger branch with counters from several different banks all available in one place. Unfortunately this idea never came to anything. It now seems that it will fall to the similarly-threatened Post Office branches to provide some modicum of banking services, especially in rural areas. However, at small local shops with limited staff it is doubtful that customers will be able to do much more than deposit or withdraw money and pay utility bills.

In 1998, Egg Bank launched in the UK. It was notable for being the first bank in Britain that could only be accessed online (or via telephone). At the time, the major high street banks were not sure if there was sufficient demand from customers for online banking, given that less than a quarter of people at that time had a PC in their homes and even fewer had Internet access. Egg gained a lot of attention initially, it offered far better rates than the other banks could, indeed, it initially operated using a loss-leader strategy. Over a period of about a decade it gradually lost steam and sold itself off, finally ceasing to exist in 2011.

Now the landscape has changed. All the major high street banks have a strong online presence, PCs and Internet access are commonplace and online banking seems to have passed a tipping point. A new crop of 'neo-banks' are preparing to open in the UK. They are online-only again, with some like Atom only being accessible through an app. They are taking advantage of new regulations introduced which make it easier for such entities to be created and in most cases are run by people who previously worked on the online presence for the big banks.

Coming at a time when banks are still suffering the effects on their reputation from their perceived involvement in the financial crisis and distaste over the size of bonuses they continue to award, this new crop of neobanks stand a good chance of gaining ground, especially since they have been able to be become approved by the Financial Conduct Authority.

Previously, this process took several years, resulting in only one new bank, Metro, opening in the last century. Now the FCA promises to process applications in 6 months. In the UK at least, it has never been easier to change bank account, with many offering a switching bonus and all able to take care of the process of shifting recurring bills without any involvement from the customer.

As with other startups busy grabbing market share in a new area, it seems likely that there are going to be several casualties before a single winner emerges. Even without the financial burden of physical branches and staff, starting a new bank is an expensive process and can take considerable time to properly establish. While they may be able to raise impressive amounts of capital, time is not on the side of today's startups, with impatient backers looking for a return after only a few years. Consumers are understandably wary about placing their money in the hands of unproven companies, even those backed by government safeguards, and since each account holder is only likely to conduct business with one provider, plenty of cash is going to be spent trying to lure people in quickly and in high numbers.

The rush to get everything online threatens to adversely affect the 17% of the population who currently have no access to the Internet, either through lack of money, interest or knowledge. Crucially, the same group of people who cannot access online services easily are quite often the same group who may be the heaviest users of public services. For most people with stable jobs and sufficient income every month, few services will need to be accessed on perhaps anything more than an annual basis.

For people who are either in and out of work or struggling to find employment, however, they may need to access services much more frequently in order to update details and claim the various allowances they are entitled to. Jobseekers may find it especially difficult as a great deal of advertisements and applications are done entirely online now, and jobseekers in the UK are required to present evidence that they have spent at least 35 hours each week looking for work in order to continue claiming benefits. If these people are surviving on very limited finances then it is perfectly possible that their only access to the Internet is through their local library, which won't have enough computers to ensure enough access for all employment seekers to spend 35 hours a week on one machine. All this comes at a time when hundreds of libraries across the UK are closing due to budget cuts. Swindon borough council announced in February 2016 that 14 of its 15 libraries would either be closed or remain open only if staffed by volunteers.

The Digital-by-Default scheme has already had one expensive setback. In early 2015, the Department for Environment Food and Rural Affairs (Defra) launched the Rural Payments System, which was a way for farmers to claim EU subsidies. It involved farmers mapping their land use and was one of the exemplar services that the government promoted as the torchbearers of digital-by-default.

Farmers had to create accounts, then log on and spend several hours attempting to get through the process of entering information about the size of their land and what it was being used for. The information required could be specific down to the size of a common garden or pathway, so estimates for how long it would take to enter all the information required for a average farm ranged from hours to days.

People who had managed to complete the arduous task (often not the farmers themselves but knowledgeable friends) said that it was beyond the capabilities of many farmers, who can easily be in their 60s or 70s, and that it was unrealistic to suddenly expect them to be able to navigate this intricate system. After several months and as many software updates, the government eventually resorted to asking farmers to go back to using the old paper forms.

Before the roll-out, the service was given a complexity rating of 8 out of 10 by the Government Digital Service. This was the highest score any of the online portals received and meant that users would need to be extremely comfortable using online tools, probably on a daily basis, to be able to use the site fully. In April of 2016 it was reported that, while all farmers were forced to use the online service, fully two thirds didn't need to. One third of farmers had no changes to make from the information kept on the old paper files and one third only had very minor updates to make.

The Rural Payments System became one of the most costly IT failures of recent times, with both a bloated budget and the real possibilities of fines from the EU due to the late filing of farm subsidy claims. It was intended as a successor to the similarly-doomed Single Payment Scheme, which ran four times over budget and resulted in farmers being paid the wrong amounts or nothing at all.

In order to connect the 7 out of 10 UK citizens over the age of 75 who have never been online, the British government intends to pay a group of 'silver sidekicks' to go into people's homes to provide training on how to access online services. This of course does nothing to mitigate the considerable cost for someone to buy all the equipment from scratch and enter into a monthly contract. And again, a huge amount of time is needed in order to become confident using the technology, especially when the first thing people are being asked to do is to enter highly personal information about themselves.

These types of initiatives should be a boon for online fraudsters, who target inexperienced users. Even the most savvy and experienced of people are occasionally caught out by a link they thought was safe or a site that is masquerading as another. It will be incredibly distressing for people to be essentially forced to spend money to get online to access a public service, only to fall prey to online criminals who may steal their money or identity.

As history has shown, the end users aren't the most likely cause of a data breach. Poor practices by the public service bodies themselves have made large swathes of data available to the open market, regardless of how careful and cautious home users have been. We can perhaps give special mention to the UK's HM Revenue and Customs who in 2007 sent two CDs through the post which contained the details of every child in the country as well as 25 million child benefit claimants. The CDs never arrived at their destination and are now somewhere out in the wild. HMRC hopes they're at the bottom of a landfill; more likely they're sat forgotten in someone's drawer. Moving forward three years and taking an equal proportion of forgiveness away, Brighton and Sussex University Hospital was slapped with a fine of £325,000 after hard drives containing sensitive patient information were found for sale on ebay. In total, 232 hard drives labeled for destruction ended up on the auction site. The government has set a target of 2020 for the National Health Service to be paper-free.

Currently, the British Government is attempting to roll out (behind schedule, over budget) a new way for people to verify their identities in order to access a range of services online which rely on the use of sensitive personal data. Similar to the Federal Cloud Credential Exchange program used in the US, gov.uk Verify, as it is known, employs third party agents like PayPal and the credit score company Experian to certify that a person is who they claim to be. The government has said that it wanted everyone to be using the system by March 2016. As of March 2015 about 50,000 people had chosen to do so. Later on that year, a report from University College London found severe flaws in the system which could lead to the possibility of undetectable impersonation of users and also mass surveillance.

If online banking shifts the problem of supplying security largely to the users, then the sheer amount of public sector data now floating around is obviously a nightmare for those who use it every day. They have suddenly found themselves to be the custodians of highly sensitive details on millions of people and are now told that they can expect to be under regular attack by those who wish to steal and exploit this data.

Many public institutions have been caught on the back foot by this and plenty of the money saved by the efficiencies of moving online have been spent on outside security consultants who attempt to bully staff into adopting a stronger security posture. Previously, data protection was part and parcel of the protection of the physical building the information was stored in and it required only minimal maintenance and no ongoing training once installed. Now the data is still thought of as being housed in hard drives in the same building, but the reality is that it is nowhere near as secure anymore and huge virtual holes exist in the walls which allow anyone determined enough to come in and take it.

Especially in areas such as healthcare, the massive benefits of a well-maintained computerized system are so obvious and apparent that there is no suggestion that things should go back to the old way. A consequence, however, is the same as that of driverless cars: it is much better to have either all cars computer controlled or none at all. Similarly, it is better to have all records digital rather than some, as this reduces the overall efficiency of the whole system and makes things more confusing for users. If they can renew vehicle tax at the click of a button, they won't be very happy with having to wait several weeks for a passport to be issued because of the time needed to manually process paper forms.

That so much of our personal details are by their very nature immutable is a problem. Each piece of data gathered can go to create an ever bigger and fuller picture of the individual. As this information is traded and sold and given away online, it only multiplies and becomes more resistant to attempts to destroy it. With each step removed data is from its source, it can be less and less obvious that it was stolen or confidential in the first place. This puts it at risk of being caught in the nets of the online trawlers that spend their days looking for tidbits about you, before becoming used by commercial entities to try and sell you hemorrhoid cream.

Both the US and the UK have very strict laws governing the reporting of data loss concerning the public. Other countries do not and so it can be difficult to get a complete picture of how bad the problem really is worldwide. When countries can keep these breaches a secret it reduces pressure that citizens would apply on the government if they knew the facts. The column inches generated by first the Snowden leaks and most recently the Panama Papers attest to this.

The common theme with the emergence of online services, whether public or private, seems to be the shifting of a burden from one party to another, the burden being typically either time, money or in many cases both. The huge influx of VC funding is also skewing the marketplace and allowing unprofitable companies with unproven ideas to run for extended periods of time. In the case of public services, it is even worse for the significant percentage for whom Internet access isn't something as standard as hot and cold running water since they have no option but to try and adapt and are not able to choose any alternative.

We see time and time again the dangers of governments and public bodies being seduced and blinded to reality by the shiny mystique of tech and all the promises it makes. When confronted by a new service they have either failed to act or been suspiciously lenient and accommodating, affording privileges which rightly irk traditional businesses.

This rush to get all our details online will no doubt coincide with an increase in the instances of data theft. This has potentially huge consequences, far beyond the problems caused by online bank fraud. Money is easily replaced and banks are insured against that type of loss. Once out in the open, however, personal information is either extremely costly and laborious or impossible to replace. The loss of a TV license number isn't the end of the world, but something like a National Insurance number, which is linked to so many things, is considerably more serious. When the data breaches do happen, and they will, they will occur on a massive scale quite possibly involving millions of records.

We are able to say with a high degree of certainty that the loss of data is inevitable because there is no such thing as a perfectly secure system and the data contained within is of such enormous value that the servers and databases will be under constant attack from those trying to profit from or otherwise exploit the information. The loss of personally identifiable information creates a whole chain of problems involving potential identity theft and the associated costs of issuing someone with new, unique information. While the British government has been digitizing records for years now, only with the prominence of the Digital by Default initiative will a large criminal element wake up to the potentially lucrative data waiting to be grabbed. Especially now that a new weak link, the public, has been introduced. It is much easier to get an ordinary citizen to click on a link which reroutes them to an infected website than it is to carry out a sophisticated attack on a heavily-defended server.

2.5 Protecting dissidents: tech vs government

Tech companies like to portray themselves as impartial and non-partisan, above the bickering of governments and the greed of corporations. They are egalitarians focused on selflessly providing the tools and services which will help shape a better world. In reality, the picture isn't quite as clear as they would like you to think and all of the major players - Google, Facebook and Yahoo have a long and complex history of supporting and opposing governments around the world as it suits their particular purpose.

For the most part, the tech world has pitted itself against governments, complaining loudly about requests for access and doing its best to increase the security of its data to make it more difficult for the authorities to monitor. What is important to remember is that both the major tech companies and major governments are actually pursuing the same goal, that is, the surveillance of citizens using these services; they are just doing it for different reasons.

It is easy for the tech companies to come out of these confrontations looking better. Most people are aware of the need for government surveillance but few people want any more than is strictly necessary - if at all. It is difficult for government agencies to sell their requests for access to a wary populace, since the only reason they can give is because they want to rifle through your private stuff, looking for any wrongdoing.

Government agencies such as the NSA and CIA are given a hugely important, terrible and quite probably impossible task: keep the citizens and the infrastructure of their country safe from terrorist attack. Despite their shadowy nature, they are subject to massive oversight and are engaged in a constant battle to protect whatever budget they are allotted from being trimmed. They are dependent on the whims of whatever party is in power at the time and are unable to publicize in a meaningful way whatever successes they have at doing their job.

Compare this with a Silicon Valley company, one with nearly unlimited resources, no oversight and an overriding ambition to, above all else, increase profits and market share. They don't have to ask to look at your data because you already agreed to let them do so when you agreed to the terms of service, that long page of gibberish that you didn't read when you created a new account.

Apple is able to brag about protecting user privacy with some conviction as the vast majority of their profits comes from hardware and sales of things like apps, music and movies. They do not have a need to trawl through your emails looking for things you might be interested in buying in the future.

After Edward Snowden revealed the scale of government spying, companies such as Cisco, Microsoft and IBM reported the loss of some big-spending customers. They responded by building data centers overseas which gave them an extra layer of protection against requests for access by American authorities. Customers are caring about where their data is kept more than ever, although due to the design of the Internet, data location can be difficult to pin down. Each day, fully 80% of the world's Internet traffic passes through the United States and is therefore accessible by the US government. However only a tiny fraction can actually be looked at, given the volume of information involved.

As a great exodus of information from American shores starts, American companies are racing to grab that info when it arrives on the other side of the ocean. IBM spent over $1bn on building overseas data centers. So important has the issue of physical geography become that new undersea cables are being laid in an attempt to keep data away from American servers.

Since the surge in popularity of home PCs started, about 20 years ago now, computing power has increased roughly in line with Moore's Law and is vastly superior to what it was even three or four years ago. Despite these advances, entry-level machines have always been described as being 'adequate for web browsing, word processing and light gaming'. As available storage space increases, so too does the size of the software applications which fill it. Games become more complex visually as graphics cards improve. Viruses are made harder to detect and erase as anti-virus software becomes better at eliminating them. This perpetual arms race extends to data transfer speeds, memory usage and cryptography, practically every facet of computing.

Recent events have shone a spotlight on the use of encryption in information technology, especially at consumer level. After the FBI requested Apple's help in unlocking the iPhone used by Syed Rizwan Farook, one of the San Bernardino killers, battle lines were quickly drawn with the majority of the tech companies siding with Apple and their refusal to weaken their products by writing a program which could help bypass the iPhone's lock screen.

There is a chance that in the very near future, debates such as this will cease to be of any importance. While government agencies such as the FBI proceed through the court system in an attempt to gain the information they want, tech companies are racing to build absolutely unbreakable encryption. If they are able to do it, then all the court orders in the world won't make any difference.

Currently, encryption comes in a variety of strengths depending on the requirement. Generally, weaker encryption is faster to implement and stronger is slower. There is no absolutely unbreakable encryption right now. Instead, there is encryption that is considered practically unbreakable; it would take so long to break it that the effort involved would outstrip the value of the information. Some encryption only needs to hold out against attack for a few hours to be considered secure. As computer power increases, they get faster at breaking encryption. However, at the same time, computers get better at applying stronger encryption so neither side gets a definitive advantage. The people creating encryption will always be in a stronger position though, as it takes dramatically longer to unencrypt something than it takes to encrypt it.

Fundamentally, encryption relies on the difficulty that computers have in factoring large prime numbers. There is no mathematical shortcut to doing it, so the computer must check every number. Given a long enough key, this may mean a single computer would require millions of years to go through all the possible combinations. Quantum computing promises computers that can very quickly work out these factors of prime numbers, so today's keys may very well be weakened to the point of uselessness. More importantly, it would mean that quantum keys could be made which are absolutely uncrackable, no matter how much time a machine had.

Another consequence could be that it may be possible to create information which is in certain circumstances impossible to duplicate. Of course, any material displayed on a computer may be copied or recreated, but what quantum encryption may offer is a way to guarantee that information generated and encrypted at point A remains the only copy of that data when it arrives at point B. This is interesting because it goes against every current property of electronic information, namely that there exists no original version and that it is easily copied and practically impossible to destroy. It is not a stretch to think that companies which make the vast majority of their profits from the trade in information would be very interested in a method by which they could own and control it in a way which made duplication impossible.

China launched the first satellite to feature quantum-based secure communications in August 2016. Although much of it remains theoretical, most of what is currently being written about this field suggests that it is only a matter of time before it is introduced to the consumer market.

Much of the focus of the encryption debate is centered on the use of very secure messaging applications by criminals and terrorist networks. However, a potentially large and damaging market for these services exists which is rarely the subject of much discussion, but it is one which may have a more direct effect on the lives of ordinary citizens.

Government bodies are rightly controlled by a lot of oversight, often independent. Since they are responsible for spending public money, it is a good idea to be as transparent as possible as this increases public trust and also helps to avoid corruption. A huge amount of the data generated from the normal day-to-day running of government is therefore archived in order to ensure accountability and to facilitate whatever future investigations may be necessary to ensure compliance with the law.

Given the amount of coverage that the methods and technologies employed by terrorist groups has received recently, it is not surprising that the potential benefits of anonymity and untraceability have become obvious to other people. Telegram is a messaging app which is now delivering 15 billion messages a month and attracts 350,000 new users per day. Its popularity has been helped in no small part by ISIS using it heavily, which led to dozens of news reports mentioning it. The unique selling point of Telegram is that messages can be set to self-destruct after a certain amount of time. These messages are also heavily encrypted making them difficult if not impossible to read (impossible in the timely manner discussed earlier), although several security experts have questioned the overall strength of the cryptographic process used by the app.

Recently, reports have begun to surface of overt use of this app by public officials in San Francisco as a way to avoid leaving a document trail which would automatically become part of public record. It is difficult to imagine a legitimate reason for them doing this and also worrying that bodies which should be open and accountable are already trying to circumvent established processes. Even more surprising is that they chose a quite probably cryptographically insecure application created by two Russian citizens whose last project, a social network, was seized by their government.

US politician Hillary Clinton has just emerged from a long-running investigation into her use of private email servers while Secretary of State and whether those servers may have handled classified materials. This investigation highlighted the sensitivity people have around the movement and storage of official communications. Although the FBI closed their own investigation, the report issued by the Bureau was damning in its account of Hillary Clinton's attitude to data safety. Several thousand emails were released as part of the investigation. This action exposed that Google has been active in creating tools designed to monitor and influence regime change in the Middle East.

We should be very worried about the potential for low-level corruption in government office and the subsequent difficulty in assigning guilt or proving culpability.

People are increasingly becoming aware of both the ease at which a digital trail can be reconstructed and the power of ephemeral communications, ones that self-destruct or leave no trace. The digitization of public records creates a total solution for people who are willing to exploit information for their own gain. Among companies which have reported data breaches, some 43% came from insiders acting either intentionally or negligently (about 50/50 either way). Employees have access to much more data than before, both in scope and scale, and can walk out with a complete copy of a massive database on a memory card the size of a fingernail.

So far, those behind such leaks seem to have been angry at their employers for whatever reason. In the future it is quite likely that people will come to realize just how valuable a commodity they are handling every day and how easy it would be to steal. Research suggests that a quarter of employees would be willing to steal data from their employer for as little as $5,000 and there have already been big data breaches caused by insiders that have been thwarted purely because of the honestly of the competing company that the individual has attempted to sell the information to.

An app called Cloakroom seeks to mirror the function and features of Telegram, but instead limit it purely to those working in government, specifically policymakers in Washington. Users must be verified first but are then anonymous after that. The main purpose of the app is to provide a space for people to openly discuss bills and policies and how they intend to vote. The makers hope to use to the data generated from these conversations to gain insights into why a particular bill was either supported or opposed.

Knowing that the discussions are being analyzed, however, is sure to affect the nature of the information divulged. Given the small number of users, de-anonymizing the comments would be relatively easy and it is unlikely that the true motivations of the participants will be revealed, especially if the reason is: 'I voted this bill down because my brother-in-law would lose a lot of money if it passed.'

The app has been covered in the media primarily for the kind of puerile discussions that always take place when people are given the impression of anonymity. Interesting, so-called 'thought leaders' have been given access to the platform in order to talk about their area of expertise and spread ideas. Presumably these people are chosen by those controlling the app, so it is quite likely that only people who happen to share their particular opinions will be invited. Similarly, the community as a whole is expected to largely self-moderate, but the operators can step in at any time to remove a conversation that they find objectionable. Having both access to the alleged voting intentions of politicians and influence on the opinions they are presented with is a lot of power for an unregulated app maker to wield.

With the recent leak of the Panama Papers, over two terabytes of documents detailing the use of shell companies and various other entities by wealthy individuals from around the world to avoid paying tax, there is a growing public appetite for transparency and accountability. Despite offshore tax havens being legal and operating by exploiting legal loopholes, prospective political candidates in several countries are promising to crack down on the practice and attempt to force people to repatriate their money and begin paying tax on it again.

Google's attitude to the 'disruption' of regimes and the protection of free speech would seem more benign if it were less obviously aligned to Google's own best interests. The company, along with Microsoft and Yahoo, was complicit in censoring Chinese search results at the request of the Chinese government. That China currently has around 700 million active Internet users may go some way to explaining the motivations of these companies to stifle free speech in that case. Yahoo went a step further by handing over private emails from reporter Shi Tao, who was subsequently arrested and convicted of exposing state secrets. He served 8 years in prison before being released in 2013. It is questionable how effective the Global Network Initiative, the self-regulating industry body created by the three companies in response to these scandals, can be.

Several companies have rushed to provide support for people living under the control of the strictest governments and regimes. It is for the benefit of these dissidents that ever more advanced virtual private networks (VPNs) and proxy servers are created. Now dozens of services offer end-to-end encryption of messages. These same services are of course being used by criminals and terrorists to plan and conduct ever more complex and borderless crimes.

To offer protection of communication to oppressed people, incredibly useful tools are made available to terrorists groups.

Giving someone an app which provides extremely strong encryption is a noble idea, but the kind of regimes and governments the makers are trying to protect them from probably care little for international law, and just being caught with encrypted communication would be proof enough for them of gross wrongdoing; it would then be easier to torture the information out of the prisoner rather than try to decode any data.

Human rights organizations have little if any money to spend on developing or purchasing tools which help people to avoid surveillance or monitoring by their own governments and are reliant on the voluntary contributions of individuals or companies; some VPN companies offer their service for free in the most strictly controlled places. Governments, however, have the resources to purchase software for tracking phone communication, emails and social media communications. There is much more money to be made creating tools for the regime rather than for the dissident.

Those involved in the attempted coup d'état against the Turkish state in July 2016 would have done well to research the relative strengths of the messaging apps on offer. The one they used, ByLock, was insecure enough to allow the authorities to create a fairly comprehensive map of people using it to co-ordinate their attack. The dissidents stopped using the app several months before the coup when they realized that it had been compromised by Turkish intelligence, but by then it was too late and the authorities already had a huge list of those sympathetic to the effort.

Obviously, problems are inevitable when companies with little or no experience in foreign affairs start treating geopolitical events like a mix of social experiment and videogame. The hacking collective Anonymous has managed to largely stay on the good side of public perception because their targets up until now have been ones that the majority of people are also against: ISIS, The North Korean government, paedophiles, etc. It is only a matter of time before this group starts turning their attention not to universally-loathed groups but to people or organizations who have merely been critical of online vigilantes. Comedian Sarah Silverman had her Twitter account hacked by Anonymous shortly after she said that Bernie Sanders supporters were being 'ridiculous' at the Democratic National Convention in July 2016.

The same is perfectly true of Google too, who dropped their 'don't be evil' motto in 2015 when they formed the new parent company Alphabet.

The Google algorithms, the secret sauce of their business, decides which pages appear at the top of the search results, and in what order. The usual aim is to try and present the most relevant and useful links first, so the user can quickly find the information they are searching for. Google does a number of things to try and determine a site's usefulness, not all of them public knowledge. It is perfectly possible for results to be manually altered so that information is more or less likely to be displayed. Since 2010, Google has been under investigation by the European Union for possible anticompetitive behavior. A similar investigation by the Federal Trade Commission was dropped in 2013, despite concluding that in some instances the company had acted illegally.

Google was one of the first modern companies whose name became a verb for what they did. Now, the site handles two thirds of all online searches and for many people it is the primary way in which they interact with the Internet when not using a major service such as Facebook or Twitter. A great many sites would simply die if they no longer appeared anywhere on Google's search results and this is exactly what the company has threatened to make happen to several services which complained about Google taking data from their sites.

Most of the FTC's and EU's investigations have concentrated on things like search results for shopping, where Google may give their own products prominence over others, and the way that mobile phone manufacturers must handle the Android operating system, for example preventing them from preinstalling any apps which compete with Google's own. Much less attention has been paid to the way in which Google orders its search results for other kinds of queries.

The FTC investigation that was dropped? The staff who worked on the investigation recommended that charges be filed against Google for anticompetitive practices, but were overruled. Had the lawsuit gone ahead, it would have been the biggest antitrust motion since the government famously went after Microsoft in the 90s.

The 2008 presidential campaign was the first where all the candidates attempted to engage with the voting public using social media, at that time still a more novel and unexplored resource than it is today. President Obama's mastery in exploiting this new channel to help spread his message is widely credited with being one of the deciding factors in his win. Amongst people under 25, he claimed nearly 70% of the vote. He was aided by Facebook co-founder Chris Hughes, who was one of his strategists. Facebook has algorithms of its own which decide how relevant new posts may be to each user.

There will never be another election where the candidates ignore the power of the online space, but to see a candidate so seemingly relaxed with new technology was a novelty in 2008. It is expected now, since the rest of the population has caught up, and now we must assume that there is a real potential for candidates to attempt to leverage the power offered in manipulating search results, and that we cannot trust search engines to be the neutral parties that they claim to be.

As far as we are aware, this type of scenario is still more likely to be found in a movie rather than in real life. Scarily, however, if it were to happen, it wouldn't even be the first time. Going back to the 1876 US presidential election we can see parallels of our own time in the dominance that the Western Union company enjoyed over communications in the United States. Then, they attempted to control the vote by only publishing positive stories about the candidate Rutherford B.Hayes and sharing with him telegrams sent by his opponent's staff. Thankfully, a search for 'google influence elections' doesn't return zero results or cause your PC to die, so it proves that they remain impartial. Or maybe that's what they want you to think...

One of the metrics which Google uses to determine a site's ranking is its perceived popularity, the thinking being that a site with lots of traffic is more useful than one with less. They look at the amount of other sites linking to a webpage to help determine this, links acting as a kind of endorsement. That there is a huge industry devoted to search engine optimization (SEO), getting sites higher up the rankings, shows that it is possible to in effect 'game' the system. Thousands of sites exist for no other purpose than to provide links to others in order to boost their profile. In 2015, Google published a research paper describing a new way to order search results, ranking them based on how true or untrue they were. Google would compare the text of a site to databases of known facts and favor sites with more factually correct information.

However, there are facts and there are facts. Some things - the capital of France - aren't open to debate, while others are hotly contested. The new Google technology uses the opinion of the majority to determine the relative truthfulness of things that aren't so cut and dried. This has the possibility to help reduce the persistence of misinformation that plagues the Internet: the link between vaccinations and autism, President Obama's citizenship, etc. Given that it will be computers, not people, that are doing the fact checking, two things are all but guaranteed to happen. The first is errors and the second is misinformation made fact by people again exploiting the system. When the majority of people use and trust a single source for information discovery, it poses a real danger of homogenizing that information and removing the many shades of grey that exist between true and false.

President Obama's 2008 campaign was very open about its use of technology, especially social media, in connecting with potential voters. Now that the novelty of this approach has worn off, the role of tech in politics is becoming quieter and more opaque. Senator Hillary Clinton's 2016 campaign is interesting in its own approach to the use of online information gathering. This arm of her strategy is being run by a startup called The Groundwork, which was backed by Google chief exec Eric Schmidt. Its primary purpose seems to be getting Senator Clinton into the White House. It is one of the biggest companies billing the campaign and employs a host of people who worked with the Obama administration. It does not publicize what it does in any specific way, but reports suggest that it is intended to replicate the kind of engagement with young voters that Barack Obama enjoyed in 2008. It would seem from early voting results that there is more involved in appealing to a certain age demographic, however, as until he pulled out, Bernie Saunders led in the under-45s category, with Clinton remaining popular amongst people who have traditionally supported her in the past.

Part of the reason for this may be that people, in all their complexity, cannot currently be reduced to a set of figures on a spreadsheet. The data engineers working for Clinton are in the business of putting people into categories but despite the amount of information we all put online about ourselves every day, it is not a complete picture. Amongst a group of female voters who may be similar in almost every other respect, some may either support or not support Senator Clinton purely because she chose to remain with her husband after news of his infidelity was made public. There may be a million other reasons, conscious or otherwise, why someone will give their vote to a particular candidate; policy may be the least of it.

The Groundwork and the project created for the Obama campaign, Narwhal, uses data pulled in from a huge number of sources in order to send out highly targeted ads to certain demographics. In the past, ads were targeted fairly broadly and lots of money was wasted showing political messages to die-hards who were never going to change their mind. The US presidential elections are often decided by a number of swing states that have no historical allegiance to one party or the other. The majority of states take decades to change and it is often seen as wasteful for candidates to spend serious amounts of time in places that aren't friendly to them. Similarly, states with a long track record of support can more often than not be relied on to vote how they have done previously. We can be sure that the Groundwork team are very interested in the lives of those living in the swing states.

2.6 Just a platform: shifting the blame

That computers don't care can be either a positive or a negative depending on how you look at it. When it comes to directing the petabytes of information that slosh around the Internet every day, the equipment which sends the data on its way currently doesn't care where the data came from or where it is going. This impartiality, we are often told, is one of the foundations of the 'fair' and 'egalitarian' Internet which we currently enjoy. Some companies would like to pay money to have their traffic prioritized over others. There is strong opposition to this with claims of the creation of a two-tier Internet, deepening the us and them divide.

In actuality, some companies already get preferential treatment for their data over others, just not in terms of speed. Many of the big companies have deals in certain countries and with certain Internet service providers (ISPs) which classifies them as 'zero-rated', which means that data coming from or going to Google or Facebook doesn't count towards whatever monthly usage limits may be imposed on customers. The stated intention of this is to provide users in developing countries, who may have severely limited Internet connectivity, a way to access sites without worry. Importantly, knowing that Wikipedia is zero-rated means that a user is much more likely to use that site over a similar service.

The movie streaming service Netflix, which accounts for around 37% of peak time Internet traffic in the US, has been a vocal supporter of net neutrality. If competitors were able to pay to have their videos sent to customers faster than Netflix could, then they could quickly lose customers who were fed up waiting for videos to buffer. However, a minute of HD video can be over 100MB, so many users with capped access to the Internet can't use the service for fear of incurring extra charges. In March 2015 it was reported that Netflix had struck a deal with an Australian ISP to have its service zero-rated ahead of a nationwide launch.

So while most of the major companies claim to support neutrality, in reality they are actively involved in prioritizing their service. This goes for more than just the data zipping along the wires. The tech companies have a long record of using the concept of neutrality to shirk responsibility towards the use of their services.

Online message boards and chatrooms are often portrayed as the spawning ground for some of the worst behavior and opinions to come from the online space. They allow like-minded people to come together under the protection of anonymity and say whatever is on their mind. This can often take the forms of attacks against an individual or group of people. Two of the most notorious sites are 4chan, founded in 2003 by Christopher Poole, and Reddit, created in 2005 by Steve Huffman and Alexis Ohanian. Both sites have a long history of flip-flopping between distancing themselves from user behavior and actively censoring user-generated content. 4chan initially operated as a place for extreme free speech and hosted discussions and image sharing on exactly the kind of subjects anyone would expect to find on an uncensored board. Poole has said regarding censorship of the site that 'the power lies in the community to dictate its own standards'.

The site came to public attention after harassment campaigns against female gamers, organized on the messageboard, were heavily reported in the trade media. 4chan quickly became synonymous with the dark side of the Internet due to users being able to post messages without registering first, offering them some level of anonymity. As the site came under increasing scrutiny for what was going on there, the policy for moderators was changed, meaning that they at least had to register with a real identity. Despite being one of the most active messageboards on the Internet and entirely reliant on moderators to weed out the very worst material routinely posted there, the position was entirely voluntary and unpaid. With each attempt to enforce even the bare minimum of conduct standards on the site, similar boards quickly appeared aping the structure of 4chan but being a place for those annoyed about rule changes. Many expressed disappointment that Poole, after selling the site in 2015, was hired by Google.

Reddit, which was bought by Conde Nast Publications in 2006, has a more legitimate appearance. It uses the same moderator structure as 4chan but in the past has taken more overt steps at controlling what content can be posted there. Efforts made at enforcing rules typically descend into pointless arguments about First Amendment rights and the site has a confusing, opaque outlook on what is and isn't acceptable. It is currently the 25th most-visited website in the world. In late 2014, Ellen Pao was brought in to take over the running of the company and given two perhaps contradictory tasks: increase the userbase and clean up the worst of the material posted there.

After banning five groups (by no means the worst five), she was subjected to a organized campaign of hatred, intent on getting her out of the job. 8 months after her arrival, exhausted by the unending barrage of harassment she faced every day from the Reddit userbase, she left the company.

As powerful as the big companies are, they are all slaves to the twin masters of profit and expansion. To keep growing at a rate which makes investors take notice, they must look abroad to new markets. The biggest potential sources right now of new users are in India and China. Facebook was on the receiving end of an unexpected 'thanks but no thanks' from the Indian government when it attempted to bring internet.org to the country. This scheme, sometimes mistakenly thought of as a charity but really just a business arm of Facebook's, was an attempt to bring a cut-down version of the Internet to people in developing countries who would otherwise have no Internet at all. It would be free and include things like Facebook (obviously), Wikipedia, BBC News, etc. The sites are curated by Facebook, which also didn't choose to explain why services were or weren't included.

While Mark Zuckerberg may be right when he says that some Internet is better than none, many were rightly skeptical of him acting as gatekeeper and saw it as a cynical ploy to boost Facebook user numbers. Evidence suggested that instead of being disadvantaged people's first experience of the online world it was instead being used as a fallback by savvy but cash-strapped customers who'd burned through their data allowance watching cat videos on YouTube. Local telecoms operators were also footing the bill for this free service but seemed not to mind as it was an effective way to gain an advantage over their rivals.

Mr.Zuckerberg holds a lofty opinion of the importance of the Internet and its place in the world, arguing that it is an essential human right. He sees getting everyone in the world online as a way of balancing out the massive wealth imbalance which is currently widening by the day (he is currently the 6th richest person on the planet). The key to the rest of us catching up to him it seems is the distribution of knowledge and information. Of the difference between the industrial economy and the online one, he said 'If you own an oil field, I cannot go in that same oil field.' It is easy, however, to think of this differently in terms of Facebook's dominance of the social media scene. If you own a user, then I can't also own that same user. There are finite people with finite time and these users would be extremely reluctant to move to a different social media site if their friends and family were still using Facebook.

Mr.Zuckerberg also perhaps oversells the transformative power of the Internet and what it is capable of, especially in developing countries. Bill Gates, once the sweater-clad poster boy of all things tech and who spent his career extolling the virtues of the microchip, soberly reminded everyone that the Internet is of little use to people living in the very worst conditions, who have more pressing issues than playing Minecraft. He has been pouring lots of money and time into trying to find solutions to immediate problems such as sanitation, safe drinking water and vaccinations against preventable disease.

There is a danger that those in Silicon Valley are unable to see the people behind the data sets that they love to work with and that they may treat the problems faced by those in developing countries as something halfway between simulation game and social experiment.

A 2015 study came to the startling conclusion that it was possible for Google to have enough of an effect on undecided voters that they could determine the outcome of up to 25% of national elections. At its most basic, if a person searches for 'Hillary Clinton', Google gets to decide whether they see stories about the scandal surrounding the Benghazi attack, or her record on promoting LGBT rights. What is displayed can have a huge and measurable impact on undecided voters. The researchers found that it wasn't just a matter of what was on the first page, but also the order they were displayed in. When negative stories appeared in the top 10 results alongside the positive ones, it made the positive ones seem more credible because the search results as a whole came across as more neutral.

Billboards and TV ads are very overt forms of vote influencing and when a person sees such an ad, they are well aware that it has come from the campaign or a campaign supporter. Search results are unlike advertisements in that they are presented more often than not as facts, popular sources of credible information which we ourselves have sought out. People are much more likely to be swayed by something if they are under the impression that they looked for the information and not the other way around. People are naturally skeptical of things sold in infomercials or through adverts in the back of magazines, but a few positive reviews of a product on an Amazon page is usually enough to make a shopper feel comfortable with making a purchase.

While it is true TV news can be very biased towards one candidate or another, the viewing public makes a choice about which channel they watch. Many people would struggle to name a search engine that wasn't Google, Bing or Yahoo. In the case of Yahoo, they now use Google's technology to populate their own search results.

Critics fear that, given how much Google may be able to silently influence the voting public, it would be very difficult for a political leader hoping for re-election to become publicly involved in trying reign in Google's power, or even openly support any policies which the company was against. Interestingly, the study into voter control also mentioned the possibility of it being done unintentionally. The Google engineers are continually making minor adjustments to the algorithms (around 600 times a year) in an attempt to return the best search results. Whether they are aware of it or not, there is a chance that their own political prejudices could have an effect on their work.

This exact practice was exposed by several journalists who were subcontracted to work at Facebook, helping to curate the site's news feed. They claimed that conservative-leaning news was regularly omitted from Facebook's front page, even if a story was trending amongst users. Similarly, some stories were purposefully placed on the front page, less as a reflection of how popular they were but rather due to direct pressure from higher-ups. The journalists involved in this work claimed that the absence of right-wing news was not the result of any kind of policy, but rather individual bias.

Google employees were second only to Microsoft's in terms of campaign contributions to President Obama in the 2012 campaign. Their lobbyists visited the White House over 200 times in the run up to the vote. On election night, Google chief executive Eric Schmidt was working in the President's campaign office on a voter turnout system intended to get the president re-elected.

Newspapers will be the first to tell you of the profound effect that the arrival of the Internet has had on their business. The last decade has seen some high profile casualties as people increasingly rely on the immediacy of the Internet as their primary source of information on global goings-on. The more forward-thinking papers launched successful online portals which in some cases have replaced or become far more popular than the print edition.

As a society, we have been conditioned to trust most of what is written down, apart from obvious exceptions. In the early days of the printing press, both access to books and the education necessary to read them was a rare thing, so the books themselves and the knowledge contained within was highly valued. This sense of importance has carried over even as, in the developed world, books are accessible to all, as are the literacy skills needed. We now live in a world where written material can be generated by anyone at no cost, yet we still seem to lend weight to anything presented in written form, be it on paper or on a screen.

Along with the newspapers that successfully moved online, there are any number of other sites that present news stories on every imaginable subject to readers who consume it as quickly as it can be written. These sites are in constant competition as readers can be as fickle as they like with their attentions and have no need to use only one, or the same site again and again as their source of information. The most basic feature of the Internet, the hyperlink, is designed solely to take people away from one place and toward another.

Journalists were one of the first groups to experience their Uber moment, before that company was even created. As soon as it became possible to publish on the web without having to know anything about the underlying website code, then anyone could do it.

Newspapers, like taxi companies, had a loosely defined maximum and minimum size in terms of circulation, and they employed the number of staff necessary to fill each days issue. There was a limit to the number of journalists' jobs and the papers could compete with one another in the depth and quality of their reporting. Accuracy and accountability became selling points. A papers political leaning played a huge role obviously, but the ones at the top were rightly lauded for their impeccable record of journalistic integrity.

Now, anyone can decide to become a journalist, just like anyone can decide to be a taxi driver. You can be a journalist full-time, once a month, anytime. Printed papers had size limitations imposed by people's attention span and the cost to produce them versus what people were willing to pay. Apart from slow news days, this meant that news and articles were competing against one another for space and the difficult job of the editorial team was deciding how much weight to give a particular story each issue. There are no size limitations anymore, there can never be enough content produced to meet potential demand. No editor of an online news site would ever say, 'I think we've got enough stories now, thanks.' There is zero additional cost involved in publishing another story.

Because of the number of people calling themselves journalists, it is inevitable that quality will decline. Such is the voracious market for new articles that demand almost outstrips supply, but because the content itself is of little importance, as long as it engages the reader for a few minutes and keeps them on the site, the rewards for the content creators are pretty pitiful.

Some high profile sites do indeed strive to mirror their traditional counterparts and require high standards of those who write for them and, as an organization, hold themselves to considerable scrutiny. This requires a large amount of effort and a large amount of money and for every site with a reputation for good quality journalism, Salon or Slate, there are a hundred whose only criteria is that it be attention-grabbing, entertaining and readable in five minutes. There is a huge amount of regurgitation with the same trivia and rumors being rewritten and republished time and time again.

The main problem with the barrier to entry being so low is that there is no longer any kind of structure in place to ensure the integrity and accuracy of much of the work published online. Clickbait sites that pay a pittance to the people trawling the content mill jobs boards wouldn't think about fact-checking anything that was sent to them, as long as it didn't make an obviously libelous claim.

Once something is published online, it is quickly copied and republished. The more this happens, the more the original claims become accepted fact and the more difficult it can be to trace the story back to its original source.

The global nature of the Internet has rendered obsolete, even if some don't want to admit it, many of the libel laws put in place to protect people from unverified, gossipy stories. The newspaper industry as a whole now operates to the same standards as the lowest publisher, since once it becomes known that major outlets are not reporting on something, people can quickly seek out the site that is.

Stories can gain traction without any influence from the established news sites. Things are liked and forwarded and spread through social media. This can be the first that a major outlet knows of a story. The stories can have an extremely short shelf life but long-lasting ramifications for those involved. Usually the story stems from a few seconds of poorly shot video captured on a mobile phone that shows some kind of outrage being committed against a person, based on either their gender, race or sexual orientation. The antagonist in the story is quickly identified and located, then subject to a few days' worth of vitriolic outpouring from people online before the story is quickly replaced by the next one.

In times of crisis, the standards can be lowered even further as a torrent of information is suddenly unleashed on the world and the news sites struggle to make sense of it all. Very quickly a massive amount of content can be generated from citizen reporters and it is not uncommon at all for things to be mis-reported, either accidentally or as a result of intentional lies. The dangers of this situation were demonstrated in the wake of the 2013 Boston bombings. Prompted by no individual or terrorist group taking responsibility for the attack, Internet users quickly turned amateur detective and began to pool their knowledge on sites such as 4chan and Reddit. Despite starting out with good intentions and an attempt at setting and enforcing rules, the forums soon turned into a frantic exchange of rumor and theory. They also became a prime source of information for journalists on both TV and in print. Off the back of this, the New York Post quickly published a photo of two men on the cover of their paper stating that they were wanted for questioning by the FBI. The FBI had made no such statement and had already eliminated the two as potential suspects.

Although the NY Post eventually paid an undisclosed amount in damages to the two men, for those who took part in what was later described as a witch-hunt, there was no kind of redress. In their defense, a group of like-minded individuals wildly swapping stories and making evidence fit their own theories wasn't in itself a danger. When legitimate news sources began to report using information taken from the forum and retweeting tips, then it quickly lent the unsubstantiated information legitimacy.

The 'bag men' cover certainly wasn't the only false story to come out of that day. Several photos taken amidst the carnage were soon being circulated around social media with dramatic, heart-wrenching captions that were all later proven to be utterly false.

Critics claim that newspapers, like every other industry undergoing massive change and the threat of obsolescence, have failed to innovate and adapt to modern society. They point to the immediacy of Internet news versus the relative slowness of the printed paper.

It can be exactly this limitation in speed which aids the development and reporting of a story, allowing journalists time to put together a fuller picture of what is happening. As far as investigative journalism goes, it is much less effective and efficient to have a large amount of people working independently than having a group which has the considerable resources of a newspaper organization backing it.

Several papers have experimented with putting their content behind paywalls. Some continue to do so while others abandoned the experiment after an insufficient number of users signed up. As print revenue declines, budgets are cut and staff let go. The reduction in staff lowers the overall quality of the journalism, which turns readers away, reducing circulation even more. The revenue from online ads is becoming more important to news sites than money from their printed counterparts, and with 198 million Internet users using ad-blocking software, there is a real war being wages for clicks and eyeballs.

In an age where people look outward more than ever, as likely to read about what is happening on another continent as their own town, we still need journalists both to filter out the increasing amount of noise which surrounds every story and to shed light on actions which may otherwise go unnoticed.

Mark Zuckerberg is particularly vocal on the concept of togetherness. He wants to draw all of Earth's inhabitants together and seems convinced that the boundaries between us, whether geographical, political or religious, are the cause of many of the problems that we currently face. Although a nice idea, it ignores the complexity of the situation, simplifying a huge number of deeply historical and connected factors, concluding that if we are all locked in a room together then we'll naturally sort everything out.

There is scant evidence that the digital utopia is having the desired effect. People are likely to seek out others who share the same views they already have, rather than seeking out opinions which challenge their own beliefs. The anonymity of the Internet allows horribly venomous attacks to be made against those with different values.

The world was given a dramatic lesson of the power of social media during the Arab Spring, the protest movement which started in late 2010 and resulted in the rulers of four Middle-East countries being unseated and civil uprisings in many more. Four years on from the end of the movement, some are questioning not only the real role that technology played in the campaign, but also if it directly led to the formation and dominance of the ISIS terrorist network.

There have been similar uprisings in the past of course, ones which came to life without the use of today's tools. It is commonly agreed that, given the state of affairs in places such as Tunisia at the time, something would have eventually happened; it may just be that social media made it quicker and easier. The two main influences which social media had on the movement were on public opinion and public organization. Instead of relying on word of mouth stories on what the regimes were up to, people could view firsthand video of various atrocities being carried out against fellow citizens.

Despite the often harrowing nature of the footage, people realized the importance of not turning a blind eye to what was happening in their own country. In many of the nations affected, the use of the Internet was heavy controlled, but the governments were no match for a generation hungry for access to information and who quickly developed the skills necessary to get around whatever blocks were in place. Once online, people could then be coordinated, instructed to be at a certain place at a certain time so as to maximize the impact of their actions.

Tahrir Square became the focal point of the world's attention in January 2011. The Egyptian government attempted to prevent citizens from accessing the Internet altogether but by this point, with so much media coverage centered on one place, it was too late for the action to have any impact. Social media had helped awaken the people to the realities of what was happening in their country and it had mobilized them to march on the square, where thousands remained for 18 days until the president, Hosni Mubarak, ceded power.

The initial wave of unprecedented optimism soon gave way to reality as a power struggle emerged after the president left with Mubarak's successor, Mohamed Morsi, removed from power after little more than a year in a coup d'état. In 2014, Abdel Fattah el-Sisi, head of the Egyptian armed forces, was elected president. During this period, thousands of people, mainly civilians and journalists, were killed by the armed forces. During the occupation of Tahrir Square, hundreds of women were subjected to serious sexual assaults.

This rapid destabilizing of the government, with confusion over who should take over and protracted voting proceedings, played out in scores of countries in the region, created an ideal situation for terrorist groups, who were able to take advantage of the power vacuum.

They had also learned of the enormous potential of social media and how it could be used for their own gain. As a direct result of the Arab Spring, a great many prisoners were suddenly released. Often this was an intentional step taken by those in power with a desire to flee, who could do so more easily amid the chaos it caused. Unprepared prison staff fled their posts and once some inmates were free, they were able to return and attack prisons in order to free others. The countries involved were notorious for their willingness to incarcerate entirely innocent people who had dared to speak out against their governments, so the large-scale release of inmates was seen as a positive step towards a more democratic and fair society. Along with harmless dissidents, however, were scores of Islamic extremists and jihadists.

Now, governments around the world are actively engaged in what is commonly referred to as cyber-warfare with the most active terrorist networks. Groups like ISIS use whatever social media channels they can to help spread their message and boost their numbers. Several citizens of European countries have traveled to Syria to join their struggle after being recruited online. The terror groups have members who spend all their time online, fostering friendships with vulnerable people and slowly building trust over a period of months before helping them arrange travel to the Middle East. The lucky ones soon realize the terrible mistake they've made and are able to escape; others are killed either by government forces or the very jihadists who they have given up their old lives to join.

When people are artificially brought together, ideas which may have previously been confined to a small group are suddenly given the opportunity to spread unchecked and this can result in a frighteningly mob-like atmosphere. Almost every day social media zeroes in on someone who has transgressed in some way in real life and is for a short but terrible time the focus of an intense campaign of harassment and hate.

While the odds seem to be stacked in the favor of citizens when it comes to using technology to bring about societal change, the governments that have been previously left scrambling to simply turn off Internet access are becoming wiser to the game too. A huge economy exists supplying governments with the tools they need to monitor their citizens. While the US argues about Apple refusing to unlock a single iPhone, American companies like Narus, a subsidiary of Boeing, creates and sells digital tools capable of mass-analyzing communications. They sold software to Hosni Mubarak when he was still in power which allowed his government to identify individuals involved in spreading dissent. They've also sold software to other notably repressive places such as Saudi Arabia. Potentially, there is a lot more money to be made from selling to governments than from selling to people who oppose those governments. The companies profiting from this are often large and not at all well known.

As unpopular as the feared government security services were, especially with human rights groups, it is now becoming clear that the same hardline forces which locked up and tortured innocent civilians were also responsible for preventing terrorist networks from growing beyond control. The regimes were far more effective at counter-terrorism than Western countries could ever hope to be, leading some to speculate that perhaps a 'better the devil you know' situation is preferable in the short term to having a democratically-elected government incapable of destroying terrorist networks, something rulers such as Saddam Hussein and Muammar Gaddafi were able to easily and ruthlessly achieve.

One of the big advances promised after the arrival of the Internet was the complete democratization of information. Anyone anywhere would be able to access a world of content, regardless of their physical location. Very quickly, however, we have seen efforts made to limit what people have access to and control the ownership of the endless spew of data that pours out of our screens every day.

2.7 The new state of ownership: you don't own anything

Silicon Valley firms have made the decision themselves to use encryption and provide it as a default service to their users. As well as the design decisions regarding user experience and product handling, high level security is sold to users as a must-have feature. For any online service, the data is the single most valuable thing they handle. Without the customer data they are nothing. Everything else they offer is secondary to the information which they hold about their customers, which is why they encrypt it. The widespread loss of customer data would be catastrophic. Many companies have lost the credit card details of their customers; this is of far less significance to the organizations since a credit card tells them very little about their users. So commonplace are these big data breaches that it doesn't have a hugely damaging effect on the companies involved.

Many more people than before are now conscious of the fact that when using a free online service such as Google or Facebook, they are the product and the reason Google and Facebook can be amongst the biggest companies in the world without charging their users a penny is that they are trading in user information, regardless of privacy settings they may choose. Advertisers spend billions each year to put adverts on the screens of the users and you can be sure that they are not just hoping that Bob Smith happens to be thinking about buying a new car.

Quite often, the flow of personal information from user to service can be hard to visualize and quantify, since the process largely happens in the background and is invisible to the user. Some gadgets, like fitness trackers, are fairly explicit in what they do since their entire purpose is to measure and track things. 2016 has seen an explosion in public awareness of virtual reality (VR) as a possible mainstream entertainment tool. Far from the bulky headsets of the early 90s, these are sleek devices which can truly claim to create immersive experiences.

The company which got the ball rolling on this second generation of VR technology is Oculus, which was bought by Facebook shortly after it made public its planned VR headset. In April 2016 it found itself on the receiving end of pointed questions from Senator Al Franken as to exactly what kind of information the headsets were collecting from users and how the company was intending to use that information.

Facebook makes 95% of its income from advertising, and few gaming companies make serious money from hardware sales, instead recouping their money from software. The Oculus terms and conditions explain that the device will collect personally-identifiable information for the purpose of showing you adverts from both Facebook and other companies. The Oculus is an 'always on' device, so there is a perpetual trickle of information being fed back to Facebook even when you aren't using it. Adverts are far more targeted today than they were a few years ago, however there is growing feeling amongst the ad industry that their money isn't being spent effectively. Many ads are never seen by human beings, instead being viewed by computers in an attempt to game the system and extract more cash from those placing the ads.

When ads do end up on someone's screen, the advertiser has no idea (unless the person clicks on it) whether it caught their eye or not, and if so, what part of it did they look at and for how long. By using the eye tracking capabilities of the Oculus Rift headset, advertisers can know both where you looked and for how long. Very quickly they can conclude that J.Jones nearly always pays attention to ads featuring a busty model in them, he stares at the model's chest for an average of 6.55 seconds and is most interested in breasts between cup sizes C and E. If you thought that your history list was about as embarrassing as it could get then think again.

In 2014, Google bought a company called Revolv, a maker of home automation products. One of the items it sold was a smart hub which helped people control all the various Internet-connected objects in their homes: lightswitches, alarms, etc. In April 2016 Google announced that it was disbanding the company and ceasing support for its products. In this case ceasing support meant that the home hub would completely stop working, since it relied on servers owned and maintained by Revolv to function. Although the userbase for this product was small and it hadn't been on sale since the company was acquired, both users and nonusers were outraged that a company could reach into the homes of people who'd paid $300 for a product and render it completely useless.

It has ignited debate on the true ownership of products in the age of the 'Internet of things', a technological movement which is attempting to hook all manner of appliances up to the Internet, from fridges to kettles and door alarms. Many of these things rely on the manufacturers to keep them going. The terms and conditions for the Oculus Rift also mention that they are allowed to deactivate a user's account anytime and for any reason; doing this would render the headset inoperable.

Recently, a $150 Internet-connected pet feeder left lots of animals hungry when the servers which controlled the device went down for around 10 hours. The product maker, PetNet, sent out an email asking users to make sure that their pets were fed 'manually' until the problem was resolved.

The biggest defense which these data-gobbling companies enjoy is that there is such a long and well-documented history of people falsely proclaiming that Big Brother was taking over the world that the notion has been largely discredited. The main threat to people's liberty was shadowy organizations or corrupt governments which would use the powers of mass surveillance in order to oppress people. The notion of an evil cabal working behind the scenes to enslave mankind became so ridiculous as to lose all power. The terrorist attacks of the last 20 years have shown that the world's governments struggle daily to keep a handle on what their citizens are doing. This perceived lack of threat causes people to not value their own information, since they do not think that it can be used for sufficiently bad purposes.

Google's parent company, Alphabet, has realized that just selling things like Internet-connected thermostats that they can deactivate whenever the mood strikes is a pretty small-time affair. To that end, they are working now on 'Project Sidewalk' a charming-sounding vision of the city of tomorrow, built from the ground up to take advantage of all that the information age has to offer. Obviously all the cars will be of the self-driving variety, and all the refrigerators will be the kind that can order milk for you automatically when it is running low. A group of top city planners are working on the initiative right now.

Surprisingly, it won't be built in San Francisco, although a final site hasn't been announced. The project's leaders have largely given up on trying to improve on the cities that we already have, instead opting to start over. This endeavor seems like the next logical step for those who write op-ed pieces about the frustrations of sharing living spaces with poor people who don't work in tech. Instead of putting in all the time and effort trying to gentrify somewhere and getting nothing but opposition in return, they can openly declare that tech people are indeed different and special and go off and live in a place where the only thing rarer than a homeless person would be a Wi-Fi deadzone.

In the future, we may see the Google buses running a reverse service, taking in the scores of cleaners and maintenance people needed to work behind the scenes, emptying the robot vacuum cleaners, taking the milk from the delivery drone and putting it in the fridge, etc. At 4:30, before the residents of the tech city have to see them, they can be herded back on the bus and dropped off at the outskirts of the normal, non-futuristic towns.

Before there were conversations about companies such as Uber and Airbnb sidestepping established rules and enjoying an unfair advantage as a result, a far more important decision was made, one that impacted everyone, not just taxi drivers and hotel owners. All the way back in 1996, the Communications Decency Act was created. Essentially, this act absolved websites of any responsibility regarding content uploaded by users. Without this, YouTube, Twitter and Facebook could not exist, since they would be liable for any illegal thing published through their service.

This special exemption for the online players was nearly two decades ahead of the battles being fought in courts by companies trying to prove that they have nothing to do with the industry that they are upending. Without this act, YouTube would be unable to accept the 400 hours of video it is sent every minute, since they would be liable for every second of what was published.

Most websites strive to maintain a reputation as a safe space for users, others more or less rely on their reputation for their sites being the opposite. It is much easier to adopt a strictly hands-off approach and put the burden for keeping the messageboards free of the most abhorrent material squarely at the feet of the users, who for whatever reason are happy to do this for free.

Once we progress past the material which everyone can easily agree should never be viewed by people, except those tasked with convicting the creators, we soon enter into greyer areas. Any act of extreme violence, physical, sexual or otherwise is viewed very differently when it is directly connected to a terrorist or political movement. The argument for this is that people have to know the barbarities of these groups so that an appropriate response can be formulated. If people are sufficiently outraged then they will apply pressure to their elected governments who can then take some kind of action.

All major services self-censor, but this has little to do with any legal obligations and more to do with preventing user numbers dropping.

If you were confronted by horrendously distressing imagery when you logged into Facebook, you'd probably stop using the site. To counter this, a huge and largely hidden army of people exists in the world whose sole job is to filter what makes it on to your screen. This terrible task is farmed out to agencies operating mainly in Asia, where underpaid and underrepresented workers are exposed to the absolute worst of human behavior. There is little support or counseling to help them with what they have to see for hours each day, and the companies which ultimately benefit do not want to talk about the service at all.

Peeple arrived in early 2015 and was met by a tsunami of hatred and negativity, something that the co-founders took as mere obstacles in their destined path to incredible success. The app was touted as a 'Yelp for people' allowing users to rate and review other people, the intention being that you could use it when thinking about hiring a babysitter or employee.

In its original incarnation, the app would allow users to rate people who weren't also members, so anyone at all on the planet could be made a part of this service whether they liked it or not. There was to be no way to get rid of the reviews or otherwise opt out of being included. After the almost universal condemnation from the online community, the makers disappeared for several months while they tinkered with it. In late 2015 they returned with a rather more watered-down application. Now users could only rate other people who'd signed up for the app, and negative reviews wouldn't be shown, only the positive ones.

The response this time was relief that the entire human race wouldn't be subject to the original idea, and puzzlement over why they were even bothering to continue, since it seemed so neutered as to be completely useless. In March 2016 the app finally launched. Users can write reviews about people not using the service, the review won't be ordinarily visible and the subject of the review will receive a message informing them that a review has been written and inviting them to sign up.

In a society deeply committed to monetizing practically anything, it says something that the two co-founders of Peepl, Julia Cordray and Nicole McCullough, have been able to create something so deeply despised. It seems that what they are attempting to do in the near future is to monetize bullying and hatred. Right now, negative reviews are hidden from general view, but the app makers have written about and are considering implementing something in the future called the 'truth license', a subscription service that for $1 a day, lets anyone view all the comments made about others, good and bad. If this feature goes live, then the free component of the service, the positive reviews, will be more or less classified by the makers as meaningless waffle. If you want to see the 'truth' about someone, all the nasty comments, then you'll have to pay. Like all good terms and conditions do, Peeple's absolves the company of any responsibility whatsoever for anything written on the platform, although it does grant them automatic ownership of all content created there.

It is a terrifying thought that a private citizen could be forcibly dragged into using a service such as this. If they receive a notification that there is a review about them, curiosity or sheer worry may make them sign up to find out what it is, and find out both that there is no way of removing it, and that others can pay to see it.

Free speech doesn't, and can't exist online. Each service makes decisions as to what it thinks is and isn't acceptable. Before long they have to make choices regarding imagery which is a powerful and important message to one group, and shocking and inflammatory to another. Each time a post is either allowed or deleted, they are making a politically-motivated choice, weighing up the pros and cons of censoring a particular idea, group or movement.

User content is the fuel which sites require to keep going. Twitter needs people to keep tweeting all the time, YouTube needs more videos every second, Facebook more posts. These sites rely on and actively solicit content from users, content which they then try to distance themselves from. If the unpaid army of volunteers who give away their time cleaning up the social media sites of the world were to suddenly realize that they are directly adding money to the bank accounts of those running the sites, they may decide to find something else to do. Were this to happen and site owners were forced to investigate everything being posted, then each service would quickly grind to a halt. So powerful is this world community that it allows multi-billionaire site owners to ask users to work for them for free. It also makes users think that not only are their unpaid efforts required for the service to work and for everyone to enjoy using it, but also that they have some kind of direct input into how the community operates, none of which is true.

Long a right-wing fantasy, recently serious discussion has started again weighing up the possibility of taking certain denominations of currency out of circulation. The freeze-dried food stockpilers see this as the first step to the elimination of all paper money, a move which would force citizens to use a digital equivalent, one which could be easily monitored and tracked by the government. Those behind the push see little to no use for high denomination notes such as 500 euro or $100 other than crime. Transporting large amounts of physical cash would be much more difficult if had to be done using only $20 notes.

It seems that the reasoning behind this argument has come a little late, since the majority of criminal cashflow is now done digitally, huge cases of money simply being a more dramatic and arresting image for use in films. Removing paper money would not only disrupt luddite criminals who like spending agonizing hours pointing guns at each other while someone counts huge stacks of bills, but also the informal economy, what may in the not too distant future may be thought of as the private economy.

It would be advisable for any serious criminal reading this to look into conducting the financial side of their business electronically, since it offers several distinct advantages. As I'm sure you are aware, money can be heavy and cumbersome to transport, it is fairly fragile and can be destroyed entirely, for example when the cargo plane it is on blows up, or when escaping secret agents throw handfuls of it into the street to draw crowds of people and slow the progress of criminals who are chasing them. Of course it is more impressive to have bundles of cash stacked up on pallets but technology marches on and so too must you unfortunately. Several digital solutions exist which make the transference of electronic funds essentially impossible to trace. You don't need to worry about serial numbers, fingerprints or exploding dye packs anymore.

So if the criminal element has already abandoned paper money, why are people such as Larry Summers still so intent on getting rid of it? The answer is the potentially massive impact of mobile payments, and the current slow adoption of this powerful new financial tool.

All the big players already have a mobile payment system in place, with Google and Apple being the two biggest. To use their service, customers use a compatible smartphone at the register to make a payment. On the device, the customer can select whatever credit or debit card they like, then place the smartphone within range of the reader.

Currently, although the difference can be measured in seconds, it is still more of a fuss to use your smartphone than it is cash or credit cards. You have to get your phone out, unlock it, open the app, and select the card you want to use. Depending on the phone you may also need to use the inbuilt fingerprint reader. You might get all this ready wen you're queuing and find the phone goes to sleep again before you get to the register. You might try to open the app and for whatever reason your phone decides to be busy with something else.

The recent release of contactless cards which can be used for low value purchases without having to enter a PIN represents the current fastest way to complete your transaction. In this field, credit card companies and the phone makers are not in direct competition with one another. Contactless payments aren't everywhere yet so many people still use cash for smaller transactions.

By getting their credit cards into the smartphones, the issuers are potentially gaining access to a much larger number of transactions, so do not mind paying Apple or Google a small commission on revenue they would otherwise not collect. Of course, the card issuer isn't paying the cost at all; the merchant is paying the charge, along with the rest of the money which they have to pay every time somebody uses a card in their store. This is why lots of small businesses don't accept card payments for small amounts. If mobile payments truly take off, and people suddenly find it more of a burden to dig cash out of their pockets or hand over a credit card, then the merchants will be left at the whim of what fee Apple or Google wants to tag on to the service charge, since they risk having their ability to accept mobile payments taken away if they don't agree to the new terms.

You don't have to be an end of the world daydreamer to realize that Apple, Google and now Facebook want two things from their efforts in this market. Firstly, they want a tiny but still valuable portion of the money you've given the shop. Secondly and more importantly, they want information about your shopping habits. The ease with which it is possible to 'like' things online, indicate somehow that you enjoyed some piece of information, has in some ways devalued the recommendation. People may like things without really thinking about it, especially those things recommended by friends or family.

The decision to purchase a product is perhaps the highest level of like that consumers can exhibit, since they are putting their money where their mouths are. Where Apple and Google differ is the use of user data. Apple is generating revenue from the small commission it takes from the merchants; Tim Cook says they aren't storing any information about what shoppers buy and have no interest in the data. Google on the other hand isn't taking any money from retailers and they are very interested in all the information generated while shopping. Because of this setup, Apple has to enter into agreements with banks and credit card issuers, while Google doesn't. A group known as the Merchant Customer Exchange, motivated perhaps by the thought of another middleman forcing their way into the process and levying charges on retailers, is busy working on their own system which they say will be dramatically cheaper than the current options.

Currently, the kind of Big Brother lifestyle-tracking that excites screenwriters is pretty hit and miss. Whenever I buy printer ink from Amazon, approximately every 6 months, I subsequently see adverts and receive email about ink, but only after I've made the purchase, surely the time in my life that I am the least likely to buy more ink. In Jeff Bezos' perfect world, he could access my printer status tool and check when the ink was almost but not quite done, he could view the data from my fitness tracker and guesstimate that the running shoes I bought the other year must be almost worn out given how much I've run.

It is expensive and time consuming for companies to provide data tracking for users. Once I've bought a fitness tracker, unless I pay a subscription for premium service, I'm not giving the makers any more money, yet I am still using their computing resources when I upload my stats to their servers. Data that isn't sold or otherwise exploited is wasted data from the company's point of view.

Given its age and how little it has changed over the course of its life, paper money seems like an obvious and easy target for disruptors. It is an antiquated and resource-intensive system; in the case of some small denomination coins, it can cost more to produce them than they are worth.

Paper money already lives up to many of the ideals of accessibility and openness that tech evangelists like to preach about. It is naive to think that simply eliminating paper money will abolish crime overnight while having no impact on how the ordinary citizens of the world live their lives. How we choose to spend money can be a powerful statement and the currently anonymous journey of slightly grubby notes around the world is under threat from people intent on profiting from the knowledge of how it travels.

We should question the motives of those advocating a move away from physical currency since it seems that it is impossible to switch to an all-digital financial system without giving up a huge amount of control over our own lives. If we were forced to keep our finances in banks at all times then we would be entirely at the mercy of those institutions. Many, not only those who track the path of satellites passing over their homes, see the move to eliminate the $100 as less to do with crime and more to do with gently leading us towards the removal of all paper currency. Of particular concern is the possibility of banks introducing negative interest rates, effectively charging customers for keeping money with them. Cash hoarding is reportedly on the rise in places such as Japan, where Negative Interest Rate Policy (NIRP) was brought in at the beginning of 2016 to try and convince large companies to start spending the huge stockpiles of capital they were keeping in their accounts.

Some think that Facebook will be the next to offer a way to pay for things using your smartphone and their messenger app. Users can send funds to other Facebook members already but the app also seems to support making payments in the real world. If Facebook has access to your personal social data in the form of information which users post about themselves, then their detailed financial history from payments made with their app, then the next logical step is for them to become a full financial service and start issuing their own financial products, such as credit cards.

Arguably they would be in a position to make better judgments of people's credit worthiness and thusly offer a more competitive interest rate than the major card companies whose tools for dissecting people are much more blunt.

Several European countries have already banned large cash transactions and it seems likely that the maximum will reduce again further in the future. Even Larry Summers, former Treasury Secretary, said that, 'Even better than unilateral measures in Europe would be a global agreement to stop issuing notes worth more than say $50 or $100.' While pundits picked up on the threat to the $100, it is interesting that he so casually cited the $50 as well. Indeed, he also mentioned a paper by Peter Sands which talks about the relative weights of $1 million when made up of $20 instead of high denomination notes. We're not likely to see criminals getting legitimate jobs because they find the effort of carrying two suitcases so onerous that it just isn't worth the trouble anymore and it should always be mentioned that Larry Summers serves on the boards of a number of fintech and payment companies, so stands to personally benefit greatly from the death of paper money.

Of a greater concern perhaps than our suitcase-dragging criminal kingpins are the millions of citizens consciously or otherwise involved in the grey or shadow economy. Although impossible by its very nature to measure with any certainty, reports of the amount of unpaid taxes from the kind of everyday transactions that people don't give much thought to are quite staggering, most put the figure for any given year in the high hundreds of billions of dollars. An entirely digital system would undoubtedly have a huge impact on tax collection since every transaction would be documented and impossible to deny. Quite likely it would lead to the creation of some other means of paying people for things for those who don't appreciate such a high level of monitoring by governments.

Despite several well-respected economists proposing an entirely cashless society, it may be too much to ask the human race to suddenly abandon one of its most important inventions. The physicality of money and the emotions that go along with having it and being able to see and handle it are hugely important and the roots of this system go right the way to the formation of our earliest societies. It is also easier than with most things to see the motivations and advantages for some, beyond any outdated spin about crime and cash. Being able to withdraw and keep hold of a tangible product is an important part of feeling in control of one's own life. When the entire sum of your life's labors is just a number on a screen that is at the mercy of the people whose computer the number lives on, any sense of independence is gone.

2.8 Don't ask, don't tell: scale of online crime

There is a fundamental difference in thinking between the crimes of real world and online criminals. In 1963 in Buckinghamshire, England, a 15-strong gang stole £2.6m (£49m today) from a Royal Mail train. Known as the Great Train Robbery, the story has become famous since then as the perpetrators escaped, were caught, fled, were imprisoned, moved abroad, were extradited and finally died. For 50 years the crime made its mark on British popular culture, spawning books, films and dozens of theories about exactly who was or wasn't involved. Even today names such as Ronnie Biggs live on in infamy.

In 2015, the Russian security company Kaspersky released details of an online raid against several banks which may have netted the perpetrators as much as $1bn. The Carbanak gang worked for two years, infecting dozens of online financial institutions with malware. Since news of the crime broke in February of 2015, nothing else has been written about it and there is no indication that those responsible are ever likely to be caught.

Due to the nature of the crimes, accurate figures about the number of cyber-attacks per year against major financial institutions are nearly impossible to accurately gauge, but it has been estimated that they are subject to millions of attacks annually, and are targeted four times as often as other services. If high-street bank branches were attacked multiple times every day (with a reasonable success rate) then they would be quickly forced to either close or significantly increase their level of security.

Banks are closing, but it has nothing to do with hold-ups, which seem almost comically old-fashioned now. In 2014 in the UK, 500 branches closed, double the amount of the previous year. 650 closed in 2015. Previously, a voluntary pledge by the major banking companies meant that the last branch in any town would be protected. This was scrapped in 2014 and since then nearly 300 of these 'last branches' have shut. The UK now has 145 branches per million inhabitants, compared with 430 per million in Germany and 690 in Spain.

It is undeniable that online banking is much faster and more convenient than going into a physical branch and many banks would point out that use of their online services is increasing directly in relation to customers in their physical locations dropping. What this doesn't address, however, is that a choice is being taken away from consumers and that they are being forced to both incur expense to do their banking and also put their money at greater risk of theft than before.

At a time when more and more banking is done online, and the choice for customers regarding how they interact with their banking provider is shrinking, it is worth looking at the attitudes that banks have to the massive problem of online fraud and the similarities when it comes to the shifting of burden. Pre-Internet, when all your money was stored (in theory) in the vault at the bank, there were only limited points of attack which criminals could hope to exploit. The bank itself was very well protected against a physical raid. Similarly ATMs employed technology to make them difficult to break into. Customers had to be wary when going to or coming from the bank with large amounts of cash, especially business owners who would be known to drop off takings on a Friday afternoon.

Criminals could never be sure if private houses contained any cash or not, so burglaries typically involved high value objects which could be sold on. This is inefficient from the burglar's point of view because it takes time and effort to find someone willing to buy the items, and they will undoubtedly receive much less than the item is actually worth. It is also easier to prove that objects have come into someone's possession through a robbery than it is with cash.

What online banking has done effectively is to greatly shift the onus for providing security for the money directly on to the customers themselves. In a sense, everyone using online banking is now keeping all their money at home, i.e. on their PC. There is little difference between having a PC on your desk which you use to access an online bank, and having a pile of physical money sat there. In some ways, having cash would be safer.

The banks have created a huge new network of weak points: the users. Now, in order to carry out the everyday task of banking to the same level of security as they did before, people must spend time and money not only on the IT equipment and broadband Internet connection, but also on security software and vitally on learning how to spot and avoid the myriad ways that criminals have invented to try and steal user's banking details. This security awareness in particular is burdensome because it requires constant updating as the threat evolves and becomes more sophisticated. Casual security training is not provided for people except in the case of the most prevalent methods for fraud which may occasionally get coverage in the press. Otherwise users now have to search out and learn about the tools and strategies criminals are employing. Prior to this, we weren't expected to keep abreast of the latest advances in safe-cracking or the most effective phrases to shout at bank tellers when pointing a gun at them.

In March of 2016, Sir Bernard Hogan-Howe, the UK's highest-ranking police officer, caused a minor stir by suggesting that customers who are the victims of cybercrime should not be refunded by their banks if they are found to have taken insufficient security measures regarding their online activities. Several groups, including consumer watchdogs and digital security experts, were quick to attack the Metropolitan Police Commissioner for his remarks. Sir Hogan-Howe seemed to equate poor online safety with people leaving their homes unlocked when they went to the shops. 44% of UK citizens will be victims of online fraud in their lifetime, reports suggest. It is amazing how quickly we have learned to adapt to and almost accept this fact. It would be unthinkable for us to accept a 44% rate of burglary or robbery in our lifetimes, but many victims of cybercrime only learn of it when their bank contacts them; since they use advanced methods to monitor spending habits they can quickly detect when something seems amiss.

As it remains a commonplace occurrence, the main things felt by victims are worry at not having enough to cover bills and frustration at banks which can occasionally take several weeks or longer to refund stolen money, although the majority of people receive a refund within a week. The faceless, remote nature of the crime diminishes feelings of anger or hatred towards the perpetrator. UK police investigate fewer than one out of every 100 frauds and conviction rates are similarly low: 9,000 out of three million cases.

It seems that the monthly statement, something most people don't even receive anymore, isn't sufficient for checking for suspicious activity. As good as the banks' automated means of detecting suspicious activity is, customers are expected to spend much more time poring over their online statements, something which can take much more time given how increasingly cashless our society is becoming.

Despite the backlash over Sir Hogan-Howe's comments, and rushed clarification issued by the Met, banks are already practicing a policy of refusing to refund customer who they suspect of being lax in their attitudes to security. Barclays Bank came out on top of a poll of the strictest banks for this kind of thing, their customers being four times more likely to be denied a refund compared to rivals.

Banks claim that they are trying to incentivize customers to use stronger passwords which are updated more frequently. To prod users in the right direction, they often institute a number of criteria that a password must match before it will be accepted, a mixture of upper and lowercase letters, a few numbers and special characters, no repeated letters, etc.

There is strong evidence to suggest that this type of password policy can actually result in weaker security. One reason is that people are much more likely to write down complex passwords that they can't remember, or even store them in a text file on their computer.

Wherever possible, people will try to make even complex passwords as easy as possible for them to remember. They will replace the letter 'o' with the number 'o', the letter 'e' with '3' and a' with '@'. For the creators of password-cracking software, this creates hardly any additional challenge, since the practice is so commonplace it is easy to account for. It takes a computer no extra time to check a password first with the letter 'a' then again with the symbol '@'. So using 'P@$$word' isn't really any more secure than using the often mocked but worryingly common 'password'. It is far too difficult for people to themselves generate a truly random password and then be expected to memorize it, then repeat this process with different passwords for every site that they want to use.

The issue of creating strong passwords conjures up in the minds of users the image of the lone cybercriminal, sat hunched over his keyboard for hours trying different passwords in order to get into the Smiths' account. This is not how criminals operate in the real world; going after one computer at a time is a very inefficient practice. The two main attack vectors are now phishing and credential database theft.

Phishing is when the attacker tries to lure the victim into clicking on a link which takes them to an infected website. Either the website can push some malware onto the victim's PC in the background, or it can pose as a copy of a legitimate website. The victim enters their username and password as normal and is either redirected to the actual website, or they receive some kind of bland error message.

What has happened is that the fake website has recorded the username and password entered. Password complexity has no bearing on the effectiveness of this attack.

Credential database theft is the more difficult, but certainly the more effective of the two. This is going after the master list of all the usernames and passwords which a site keeps. These lists should of course be encrypted, but that isn't always the case. In 2015, 000webhost lost 13 million plaintext user login details in an attack. Sony lost one million credentials which were again stored without any encryption. Talktalk lost 2.4 million records which included unencrypted bank and address details of their customers.

This kind of information loss is much more severe than the loss of a credit card number, which can be replaced in mere moments. Bank account details are extremely laborious to change and address details effectively impossible, so this information has a much greater useful shelf life for criminals because they know that it will remain the same for many years after the attack has happened. Credit cards must be exploited quickly to be of any use and the issuing company is capable of suspending and replacing thousands of accounts at the touch of a button.

These kind of large scale data breaches have become so commonplace now that they don't generate nearly the kind of reaction that they used to. In many cases, customers of a service don't even seem to care. In the summer of 2015, the website Ashley Madison, which primarily caters for people who want to conduct extramarital affairs, suffered a massive loss of customer data. Given the nature of the site, there seemed to be no worse thing that could happen to it. For a short period the media was awash with stories of breakups, scandals and potential suicides as a consequence of partners and spouses discovering infidelities. In the months following the attack, however, traffic to the site and use of their app actually increased. When sites become aware of a large data breach, they now reset users' passwords for them automatically instead of asking them to do so as they did previously because such a large number of people just wouldn't bother.

On an individual level, casual Internet users are most likely to suffer the effects of cybercrime. The generation which has grown up using computers and the Internet is inherently more savvy and cautious. They understand that just because their antivirus software says in big green reassuring letters 'your PC is secure', this doesn't actually mean so. Someone who has had to acquire a PC, partly because they want to use online banking, may be a lot more trusting. If the computer is telling them everything is fine, why would they suspect otherwise? Without being explicitly told so, how are they to know they may receive emails that look to be from their bank, but are not, and that they may be taken to a website that looks like their banks, but isn't? The little green lock that appears on most modern browsers next to the 'https' and is supposed to indicate that a website is secure is 16x16 pixels amongst millions on a monitor.

In terms of manhours wasted, online banking racks up a lot by asking each and every customer to have more than a passing interest in cybersecurity and to spend time researching, choosing, installing, managing and updating security software. None of which, it seems, can guarantee against users' money being stolen by a teenage hacker who has simply purchased a piece of nefarious software and isn't required to possess any level of technical expertise in order to use it. As long as the banks are seen to take it seriously, and the losses don't account for more than they are spending on protection, then the banks can keep the onus on customers to be quasi-cybersecurity experts.

The world as a whole is struggling to catch up with the new era of truly international crime, something which criminals are exploiting every day. There is as much chance that your banking details have been stolen by someone in a completely different country as by a fellow citizen.

In the same way that tech company founders like to portray themselves as aloof tinkerers rather than dedicated businessmen, there is a pervading image of online criminals being misunderstood teenage geniuses, with ample brainpower but nowhere to direct it. It certainly hasn't helped that several high profile hackers in the past have ultimately found employment with legitimate businesses based on the strength of their IT knowledge. That isn't to say that these people haven't redeemed themselves or changed their attitudes, but it perpetuates the image of people doing it for the challenge more than anything else, something which is just not true anymore. Online crime is a well-organized, extremely focused effort involving hundreds of people with different skills working together, all part of complex international webs of structured systems. Monies gained finance real-world things such as terrorist organizations.

Although the actual crime is widely reported, when it comes to definite numbers and totals regarding losses from banks to cybercrime, things aren't as transparent. In April 2015 Adrian Leppard, commissioner of City of London Police, reported at a TechUK conference that the actual figures involved are far higher than what is reported, because banks prefer to write off the stolen money as losses and operating costs. The reason behind this being the loss of a customer who moves banks because they perceive their current one to have insufficient online security is a bigger blow for a bank than theft. The theft only takes some or all of whatever money is in the account at that particular time; the loss of the customer removes all the money for all future times too. Mr. Leppard also said that only one in five cybercrimes is reported, and of those only one in five is investigated. It seems that whenever they can, banks hide losses from theft to try and avoid damage to their reputation.

Plainly, this puts customers at a huge disadvantage. Not only are they being less than gently prodded into abandoning their high street branches and going digital, but they are not given sufficient information to be able to make an informed choice about where they should bank their money. This amounts to collusion between banks and thieves. As long as the losses don't reach too high an amount, banks will help obscure the crime and take no meaningful action to pursue those responsible. It seems that banks have a huge tolerance for theft given that the amounts reported, which it is claimed are a gross underestimation, are already huge.

While private customers' money is insured against theft, many businesses' and institutions' cash isn't, and as they typically have that much more of it, they are higher value targets for cybercriminals.

Vulnerability to cybercrime can be measured in terms of attack vectors: the more vectors available, the greater the chances of success. A single home computer with the latest antivirus has a smaller number of vectors than a business with several dozen computers all with different levels of protection.

There is often a large amount of banking traffic generated within companies which makes losses more difficult to spot in a timely manner. The volume of emails and network traffic being passed around each day provides lots of opportunities for attackers to introduce malware into the system.

2.9 The hacker will see you now: medical vulnerabilities

Whether it be starting a company, radicalizing people, publishing creative works or sharing images of child sexual abuse, the Internet has lowered the barrier to entry for practically anything a person may wish to do. Anyone can blog, make a video, make an app, start a service.

A reasonably small number of people would walk into a high street shop and steal a CD or DVD. Millions, however, illegally download music and movies with barely any pause. There is a stark difference in thinking between the theft of a physical item such as a disc and the work contained on it. Similarly, fewer still would ever attempt to rob a bank, it is an almost comically old-fashioned crime now. As you read this, however, every bank in the world with an online presence is under near constant attack from people attempting to steal money.

The average high street bank in the UK holds approximately £75,000. Online bank theft (reported) in 2015 was £60m. That's 800 banks being robbed every year. One in 10 UK high street banks being completely cleaned out by men in ski masks (or nylons if they're so inclined). Amazingly, there were 847 actual bank robberies in 1992 in the UK down to 66 by 2011, but the average proceeds from a successful robbery are £20,331, with a third making nothing at all. It is questionable, however, if the same men have traded sawn-off shotguns for keyboards; that would be quite a dramatic career change for people whose options were probably limited in the first place. More likely they have joined pager salesmen and video rental shop owners around solemn pub tables as they complain about the rise of the young generation and their lack of appreciation for what things used to be like.

The average age of the burglar is rising as youngsters shun this risky and inefficient approach and instead move online. Burglary is down 69% compared to 1995. Online crime is flourishing and growing every year. Given the amount of computer screen time they are logging, there is a real risk that the current generation of thieves are going to be at greater risk of diabetes and heart disease than the previous one.

The modern Internet is built on the absolute worst foundations, underlying technology and protocols that have barely changed in the last 40 years, leaving everyone open to attack from malicious users.

The Internet as we know it was never designed to be something we all used; initially a venture of the US Department of Defense, it was intended to link far-flung military outposts.

The system was adopted by academia and soon an informal network of university campuses around the US had sprung up. The network was maintained solely by whoever it had fallen on at each institution, usually the person with the most experience of using 'the computer' each place owned. It was perfectly possible for the system administrators to know each other well in real life and also have a fairly solid knowledge of all the users on their own systems, since they were students they saw and interacted with on a daily basis. The system ran on a huge amount of trust and only the barest security measures were put in place. Such was the low volume of network traffic that admins could easily see each individual and how they were using the network, so it was easy to police.

As the number of institutions connecting to the network grew, so did the problems. One of the first documented examples of misuse closely mirrors the issues we are facing today. A user in Germany was, for several months, able to access not only the educational networks in the US but the military ones too. Through the dogged determination of the system administrator at Berkeley, the hacker was eventually caught but the case was a clear example of the difficulty of tackling cross-border crime. It was largely left to the administrator to make contact with various international police agencies and try to convince them of the potential severity of what was going on.

Fast forward 40 years and the most powerful government spies in the US are only capable of monitoring a tiny fraction of all the traffic that passes across the network every day, despite having access to huge resources. Online crime is a multi-billion dollar industry, able to survive and proliferate because the network we use today is the same one that was in use 40 years ago, simply scaled to undreamed-of size. The only time that most users were aware of the limitations of the network was around 2015 when it was well-publicized that the Internet was soon about to run out of IP addresses, the unique numerical identifiers that are essential for allowing packets of information to be correctly routed to an individual machines on the global network.

This problem was addressed, but the issue of the unsuitability of the core network principles was not, indeed quite possibly can't be. Everything that accesses the Internet does so through the common use and implementation of the same set of standards; changing this would require replacing every piece of either software or hardware in existence, not feasible at all now given how many pieces of connected equipment there are in the world.

This number is set to skyrocket in the next few years as the much-heralded Internet of Things (IoT) comes into existence. The change in addressing was so effective and forward thinking that there is essentially no way we can now run out of addresses. This means that absolutely anything can be connected to the Internet with a unique address and we no longer have to worry about overloading the system. Companies have really taken this to heart and are racing to connect every appliance they can think of to your home network. Wi-Fi kettle? Too late, somebody not only already thought of it and made it, but somebody else already hacked it and started boiling water without even being in the owner's home.

The new rash of Internet-connected devices that are starting to appear on the market place security pretty far down the list of priorities. The Internet-connected Barbie and VTech smartwatches and tablets were all quickly hacked, with the VTech toys spilling out the details of over 6 million children. In an effort to make the products easy to use for people who aren't tech experts, they often sidestep traditional security best practices.

A lot of coverage was given to the dramatic story at the end of 2015 that described websites which let anyone view the live feeds from thousands of Internet-connected baby monitor cameras that hadn't had their default security information changed. Just beginning to come in to public consciousness are websites such as Shodan, which is a search engine for IoT devices. It is a constantly updated list of webcams, routers, databases, anything at all that has been connected to the Internet in such a way as to allow connections to come in from outside (most devices do this by default). Now without any technical knowledge whatsoever, users can casually browse a world of devices never meant to be open to the public.

Computer viruses, once just an annoyance that would simply cause malicious damage and nothing else, have grown up recently. The most popular kind to emerge over the last few years is ransomware. These viruses encrypt a victims entire hard drive then demand payment in order to unlock everything again. The encryption is so strong that there is now way around it and the advice coming from law enforcement has been in most cases to just pay up if you can't bear the thought of losing the files.

It is a hugely profitable scheme and relies on the latest generation of untraceable payment systems, such as bitcoin, to allow the authors to rake in the ransoms without fear of being traced.

With the rise of IoT, it looks like ransomware will continue to grow and spread, as it is possible that soon, instead of blocking access to your home PC files, ransomware could lock you out of your Internet-connected car, mess with your Internet-connected pacemaker or switch off your Internet-connected TV.

As consumers, we are able to pick and choose which products we bring into our home and unless you are a staunch early adopter, by the time you decide to purchase a new product, most of the major threats will probably have been identified. More scary is the vulnerability of the devices which you interact with but have not specifically chosen to do so, the most potentially dangerous example being the equipment your life may depend on if you are ever admitted to hospital. These devices are being connected to the Internet with the same speed as everything else and if anything, are even more susceptible to attack than consumer-level products, since they are far rarer and it is not generally possible for white hat (non-criminal) hackers to put them through any kind of rigorous tests. A new smartwatch or fitness tracker will be pretty thoroughly torn apart by numerous independent groups of tinkerers shortly after release, but complex medical equipment can go completely untested in field conditions.

Hackers, however, are very interested in them. They can be sure that, depending on what kind of machine they attack, the hospital is extremely likely to pay up, firstly to regain access to a piece of equipment they may rely on and secondly to avoid embarrassment. A very small number of concerned citizens are currently involved in stress-testing hospital hardware against outside attack. Their task is made more difficult by both the relatively small number of people working on the problem and the difficultly and expense in getting hold of the equipment, in some cases private citizens being forbidden to own certain devices. The flaws they have found so far sound like plot devices from poorly written movies, vulnerabilities that allow them to remotely access things like infusion pumps, the device which administers drips or other drugs automatically, and make the machine inject however much they wanted in to a patient in one go, or pacemakers made to give dangerous shocks.

Medical staffs are concerned with the day-to-day operation of the machines they use. It is unfair and unrealistic to expect them to also be network security experts so that they may spot the security holes in these devices. As hospitals switch (voluntarily or otherwise) to all-digital workflows, it makes sense for equipment manufacturers to connect their devices to the same network.

It is cheap and easy to stick a network port on something and makes for a good selling point. As the researchers have seen, however, if the default configurations aren't changed then it is very easy for anyone to gain access to the devices. Patient safety seems to currently be reliant on this tiny group of independent researchers who pass their findings on to the equipment manufacturers. Often, they've found themselves ignored by these companies and have had to contact government agencies to get some kind of result. A positive outcome still then depends on the company making a fix for the problem and issuing the solution, with the final point of failure being that the hospital has to receive this information, understand its importance and be able to carry out the necessary steps.

In February 2016 Hollywood Presbyterian Medical Centre in LA was hit by a ransomware attack which demanded over $3m to unlock patient files. The effect of the attack on the hospital was so severe that some patients had to be transferred to a different facility and doctors were forced to send and receive information via fax machine. The hospital eventually paid out $17,000 in bitcoin to get the key needed to unlock the information.

A certain amount of eye rolling met the announcement of the first consumer-level refrigerators with Wi-Fi built in. Hospitals on the other hand routinely use network-connected fridges as it allows staff to monitor the temperature range and receive alerts if it falls below a certain level, absolutely essential for maintaining blood stocks. It seems that third parties can access the fridges and change the temperature to whatever they like, remembering to turn off the automatic notification before they do so of course.

Practically every device in use in the hospital requires very precise adjustment. Whether it is medicine or radiation, patients can't receive either too much or not enough of anything. Not only are the devices susceptible to interference from outside, but they can also be made to work well outside of the normal range of operation.

Although a dramatic scenario, we have thankfully yet to see a verified case of death or injury caused by malicious interference with a piece of medical equipment. For the profit-minded hacker, there are less risky and more rewarding things they can concern themselves with when virtually within the hospital walls. Private medical data is the obvious choice; plentiful, easy to transport and potentially very valuable, fetching 10 times what credit card information goes for on the digital black market.

In 2009, the US Congress approved the Health Information Technology for Economic and Clinical Health Act, a nationwide effort to digitize patient records. At the time, massive cost savings were predicted, as well as numerous benefits for patients, whose records could be updated and accessed from anywhere instantly. It has proved a costly endeavor, with medical centers having to shoulder the burden of this change and being largely at the mercy of a limited number of approved equipment providers who are able to charge what they like, sometimes selling proprietary systems which don't allow the sharing of information with rival offerings. In the early days, doctors complained of the sheer amount of time that they were being forced to interact with their computers rather than their patients.

Medical diagnosis and treatment plans are often completely unique to each patient, but this did not fit well within rigidly standardized software which forced doctors in certain cases to choose the closest thing to the patient's actual information as the program wouldn't let them enter whatever data they wanted. Similarly, reports could be auto-completed with a few clicks so medical staff began questioning the reliability of the medical information, since there was every chance that the checks which had been marked as having been carried out, weren't.

Four years after the start of the effort, less than 20% of physicians were sharing information with outside providers. Hospitals were still waiting to see any kind of return on investment, with some reporting being out of pocket not only for the cost of the equipment and services, but also because of inaccurate billing caused by problems with the new software, in some cases running to millions of dollars.

Whether as the result of deliberate attack or just classic computer personality, when the system goes down, it has major consequences for the hospital. Keeping an up to date paper system alongside the digital one would completely negate the time-saving benefits of computerization since staff would be doing double the admin that they used to do, so they are often entirely reliant on the IT systems.

Medical information is some of the most unique, personally-identifiable information that we have. When it is stolen, it can have far-reaching consequences. First and foremost there is the emotional distress to the patients, who are concerned about a total stranger knowing such personal details about them and perhaps trying to blackmail them at some point in the future. The information is often immutable, meaning that it can't be changed. The criminals can use this data for a wide variety of further crimes, chiefly medical insurance fraud.

As medical institutions and associated organizations become ever more connected, the risks of massive data loss increase. It can be costly, difficult and sometimes impractical for hospitals to follow the same kind of computer security best practices which home users do.

Given limited budgets, computer operating systems may languish for years after support has dried up and when computers are essential to the running of a 24-hour service, when are hospitals expected to find the time for a massive overhaul of their IT software, something which may take days to properly carry out?

The default attitude that computers make everything better ignores the realities of certain situations where, improperly administered, they can actively make things worse. Governments are too easy blinded by promises of massive cost savings and efficiency gains and so try and force the hand of hospitals who may otherwise maintain an if it isn't broke, don't fix it attitude to their current setup. Although we are still in the early days of this massive process of digitization, the warnings from concerned parties are already coming to pass. Patient data has been stolen, medical devices have been remotely hacked by genuinely malicious people. Patients are being put in harm's way and having choices taken away since they are not given information about the very real vulnerabilities of the equipment that may surround their hospital bed. Many worry that it is going to take a massive data breach or verifiable loss of life to really drag this issue out in to the light.

A home user is able to pick and choose which software they have on their machine. It is this choice which can make them more or less open to attack from cyber-criminals. Although it is onerous for individuals to have to maintain a baseline set of computer security skills and common sense, this freedom is important as it places a degree of control in the user's hands. With the coming age of IoT devices, this choice looks set to be removed. Users simply won't be able to tinker with their Internet-connected car or toaster in the same way that they can with their PC. Either the vendor will expressly forbid it, or there will be no simple way for the layperson to be able to do it.

This means that consumers will have to rely on the manufacturers for their day-to-day safety. I can choose to have no anti-virus programs on my PC or I can adopt an extremely strict attitude to security; that is my choice and I am aware of the pros and cons of each stance. If IoT becomes so ubiquitous in the future that it starts to come as standard, then I'm being forced to potentially open up huge holes in the security of my home IT setup, since attackers can often exploit a vulnerability in something benign and use that foothold to pivot into something bigger and more valuable in my home. The willingness of attackers to sit and try and break the security of a device will always outweigh the willingness of the manufacturers to try and make that device secure.

While credit card companies have invested huge amounts in the fight against fraud and can now boast some very advanced systems which are capable of instantly detecting suspicious activity, health insurers are far less experienced in this field.

Criminals armed with personal medical information can, however, exploit the insurance system for personal gain for much longer than they could expect to do with stolen credit card details, which may only be good for a single purchase. They may make orders for medications their victims are using and then resell them, or use their knowledge to make a false but believable claim against the victims medical insurer.

Potentially, someone could even commit identity theft and seek medical treatment using another's details. This wouldn't necessarily be the original hacker, more likely someone without health insurance who for around $20 is happy to take the risk.

Not enough pressure is being put on hardware and software makers to make their products secure. We have come to think of hackers as an inescapable part of a technologically-dependent life and there is some truth in that, since there is always another vulnerability out there waiting to be found in each product. With every security hole they close, however, manufacturers make it that much more difficult for the attackers and raise the barrier to entry, removing an entire group of people who will move on to other low-hanging fruit. If teenagers are able to steal more from a bank with a computer than armed robbers can with a shotgun, this demonstrates the ineffectiveness of the current security setup. Consumers need to start putting higher priority on the security of products in order for manufacturers to respond in kind.

2.10 (very) Top of the pops: music industry changes

For just over two years starting in June 1999, before social media, apps and smartphones, an online service starkly demonstrated the transformative power of technology on established industries. Napster, the peer-to-peer file-sharing service, brought to the public's attention the notion of illegally downloading music from the Internet. Of the thousands of articles written about it during its short (initial) lifespan, some of the more attention-grabbing foresaw an end to the recording industry and the ability of artists to generate meaningful income from their work. Fast forward 16 years and today's top musicians are able to monetize their work in a way which makes even the most famous commercial sell-outs look like amateurs in comparison. However, as with other sectors that have been reshaped by technology, we find a large and unnatural divide between the haves and have-nots.

The stereotype of the successful musician or band is of childhood passion for music, years spent struggling against adversity and obscurity, eventual overnight success then a rapid selling out of their beliefs and ideals as they become consumed by greed. Eventually they find themselves without money, a contract or fans and they begin again, humbled and once again doing it 'for the music', never to reach their previous heights but doing so with renewed credibility. This trope has been mined for comic effect in many movies and is not quite as broad as is seems. Few artists remain consistently successful their entire lives (if they don't die young) and fewer still can avoid the trappings and creative stifling of immense wealth.

Given the suddenness of Napster's prominence in the public eye and the sheer amount of media coverage it received, it is not surprising that moves were quickly made to squash it. The service was an early example of the 'we're not responsible for what people do with it' attitude that still persists to this day. The creators of Napster attempted to absolve themselves of any legal liability by saying that they didn't themselves host or distribute any music, but that users shared directly with one another; they were just the introduction agency.

Today, P2P usage has somewhat plateaued. As Internet speeds increase downloading even huge files, such as copies of Blu-Ray discs, becomes a possibility. However, the movie industry has learned from the mistakes made by the music one.

Consumers have dozens of easy, cheap and legal choices when it comes to watching films online and it has been recognized that the sums claimed to be lost to piracy each year are not a true reflection of lost sales revenue and that many pirates would not purchase the movies they download, even if piracy were eradicated overnight.

The rise of Apple's music store meant the demise of places such as Tower Records and HMV. Only a few years later, the landscape is changing once again and the concept of buying individual songs or albums as a digital download is starting to look clunky and inefficient, when once it was cutting edge. Streaming looks set to replace downloads very soon.

The biggest players in the online music streaming industry are Spotify, Apple Music and Google Play Music. Nearly all the major services charge a flat rate for unlimited streaming and have extensive catalogs. Currently the services use exclusivity as one way of competing with one another. The Beatles, for example only appear on Apple Music. YouTube is an exception to this group in that it is the only service artists cannot opt out of. YouTube allows music to be uploaded to the site by implementation of the Digital Millennium Copyright Act (DMCA) which allows for non-commercial use of copyright works. In August 2016 Universal Music Group announced that it was going to ban music released on any of its nearly 80 labels from being streamed exclusively on one service over others.

One of the core concepts touted during the Internet's sudden rise to global prominence was the idea of a truly level playing field. Artists no longer needed a record contract, they could record and upload it themselves and get it into the hands of fans the same day, a true meritocracy with bands who were genuinely popular enjoying success.

Now, instead of struggling to make a living by playing local pubs and clubs, many musicians are struggling to make a living sitting in front of their computers, wondering why the seemingly large amount of plays their songs are enjoying isn't translating into higher revenue. For an unsigned artist to earn the minimum monthly US salary of $1,260, their video must be played 700,000 times on YouTube. That 700,000 plays is enough to earn one member of the band the minimum wage; drum machines have never looked so attractive.

Musicians' attention has turned from piracy to streaming. They are locked in fierce battles with the largest providers, all of which are legitimate companies.

The music streaming services were a reaction to and an attempt to monetize piracy. Streaming is not an alternative to buying an album, it is an alternative to piracy. Realizing that it would be impossible to completely eradicate file-sharing sites and services, they instead charge users a flat fee to sidestep all the legal and moral problems associated with piracy, promising to fairly recompense the musicians whose music they provide. The damage was done by services such as Napster and Limewire, however, in that the perceived value of the product had been irrevocably harmed. People will not pay the same (and why should they) for a digital product as a physical one, and people will not suddenly start paying a lot for something which they previously enjoyed for free.

The availability of a common music market, open to everyone, should have changed the makeup of the music industry more than it has. With every artist having an equal chance, there should be a broader spectrum of people enjoying good success and far fewer megastars dominating the airwaves. The structure, however, remains much the same as it did in the heyday of MTV. Anyone can make and upload music now, but that doesn't mean that creators of good work will be recognized, either critically or financially. The main beneficiaries of the legitimizing of the online music ecosystem have been established artists, who have been able to collect money on their back catalog without the desperation of issuing another greatest hits album. Artists with small fanbases have to like it or lump it when it comes to the money they can collect from online streaming services. They are free to move to a service which offers more, but that may not necessarily translate into more earnings if that service has fewer subscribers. Listeners don't have the time, patience or money to seek out work which isn't immediately accessible.

Established artists enjoy a great amount of influence over both where their work appears and how much they are rewarded for it. Several high profile musicians have removed their music from sites because they were unhappy with the financial terms. In 2015 Taylor Swift used her considerable sway against Apple when she wrote an open letter complaining about how artists wouldn't be paid for songs played by users who were in a three month free trial period. Within hours the company reversed their position and said that artists would be paid (at a reduced rate) during the trial period. While it was seen as superstar nobly standing up for the little guy, such was Swift's popularity that the difference for her in terms of royalties during the three-month period would be substantial. She has since gone on to develop a close relationship with the service, starring in several of Apple's TV adverts.

Apart from the 16 artists on stage that night, the entire music industry groaned under the weight of pretension and artistic entitlement when the streaming service Tidal was launched in March 2015.

Touted as a solution to the problem of low rates of return for online streaming, Tidal promised to pay a fair royalty. To do this, subscribers would have to pay $20 a month, double the cost of Spotify. Whatever aspirations the service had at launch were overshadowed by the sight of some of the biggest names in the music industry coming together to get more money for themselves. Although the userbase remains comparatively low, around three million one year after launch, it has benefited from some big names, such as Beyoncé and Kanye West, making their work exclusive to the service. This unfairly punishes the listeners who either have to pay a second subscription just to hear one or two artists, or do without; it is of no benefit to the thousands of struggling musicians living paycheck to paycheck.

Alon Rodovinsky and Ivan Popov are two Toronto-based musicians who are, like many others, navigating the suddenly both accessible and labyrinthine world of media creation and promotion. The pair were high-school friends who reconnected after university and decided to pool their talents. They now split their time between creating their own music under the name Audio Insurgency, for-commission pieces, as well as the equally difficult task of attempting to have their work heard above the sea of noise generated by the maker community, both amateur and professional, which increases every day.

Alon and Ivan release their independent music on Songtradr, a platform which allows them to directly license their work, and Soundcloud, one of the biggest platforms and the one the pair have had most success with. Ivan describes the basic process, 'People can go on there and they can look up keywords and you can be put on playlists and discovered that way ... it's expected to be free but you can link people to a [website] where they can buy your stuff. The service has experimented with several different revenue models, both for themselves and for the content creators. By 2014 the company had over 250m users and was valued at $700m. Losses for the company in that year however were $44m, throwing some doubt on the long-term viability of the platform.

Both accept that the current way of doing things presents challenges but are more concerned with producing the best quality work possible over endlessly marketing themselves. When asked about how they juggle both creation and marketing, Ivan said 'promotion is not easy ... you don't want to be too annoying. When you start [promoting] you realize if you do it alone it's going to take a long time'. Alon added 'You can resent it but you shouldn't because when you're in the opening stages of any business you have to think of reasons why people would even [want] what you're selling ... when you start having a bit more clout then definitely I want to outsource as much of that as possible'.

While it is obviously wise to consider the appetite listeners have for seeing the same music promoted again and again, artists must strike a balance between following the common best practices for self-advertising and also trying to build some momentum immediately after new material has been released, as Ivan said, 'The most effective promotion comes straight after you release the track because that's how Soundcloud's metrics work, you have the biggest chance to get in to the top boards if you get listens and likes quickly ... six months down the road it's not going to get in to the charts no matter how many listens you've got.'

The pair sees part of the current problem being that there are too many streaming services, some only catering for a particular niche but all trying to steal each other's customers, who are only likely to ever pay for one provider. Interesting, in this case they suggested that less choice could potentially be beneficial, for example if

YouTube were to eventually see off all other competition. 'Its an example of a monopoly that could work.' Alon said, 'That service would get all the listens and be able to pay out the maximum amount of money to the song writers. It would be really convenient because all the songs are there, if they don't try to screw people over.'

Despite the difficulties, both seem optimistic about the future. The biggest improvement for Alon would be convincing people that it would be better to pay for their streaming rather than have it be ad supported. Ivan points to the way the PC gaming service Steam transformed the purchase and ownership of software, making it so easy that it was even able to forge a large market in Russia, somewhere infamous for rampant piracy.

Like many, their income is detrimentally affected by the huge number of plays that major artists can rack up. Of the top 10 most viewed YouTube videos, 9 are music videos and have had between 1.5 to 2.5 billion views each. At those kind of numbers, even fractions of cents add up to serious amounts, but while artists can celebrate getting to 5,000 listens on a song, they can't celebrate too hard, given the kind of returns they can expect, 'The royalties are not good. The argument being that you don't have to reproduce anything, move anything ... because it's digital, there's not much upkeep. I feel that it's really underwhelming, the amount you get back' Alon commented.

Neither has any misconceptions about the roles of streaming and piracy; for avid music fans there is just too much new work coming out all the time for those interested in discovering new material to purchase on a track by track basis. When asked about their feelings towards the general state of the market, Ivan said 'You take it as it is and you work with it, there's no point thinking of it as a positive or negative thing'.

Streaming means the artists will have little other choice but to throw their work in to a huge common pool and hope that it somehow finds an audience. The iTunes store was no different from shopping in an HMV essentially. Once the public has had their perception of music as a product altered, that is from purchasing it piece-by-piece to it being a utility like cable television, then the industry as a whole will have undergone a seismic shift.

The old P2P services dealt a huge, long-lasting blow to the music industry, but one that didn't affect prominent artists, merely put unknown acts at the mercy of a handful of large tech companies. When they first appeared, Internet speeds didn't allow for the downloading of movies, only music files which are much smaller. The iPod gave the world a way to carry around all their illegally-obtained music and there was a lack of easy ways to legally purchase music as well as a reluctance from the consumer to pay a similar price for an intangible download as for a physical product ($16 vs $10 in the case of albums and downloads). With access to the online ecosystem, musicians are now expected to be businesspeople, spending as much time managing their online presence as they do making music. What may be an exciting opportunity to some may be a loathsome chore to others.

2.11 Looking back in anger: founders take on education

With many of the ventures coming out of Silicon Valley intent on upending our lives for the better, it was easy to see the possible inspiration behind the initial idea. Unfortunately, the daily lives of those residing in that particular area of California may not be a suitable representation of life for everyone else. While San Francisco tech workers may indeed be too busy to clean their own apartments, most others aren't. They may have no idea who they are living alongside and have no idea how to knock on a door and introduce themselves, but even in this day and age most people are at least on nodding terms with their neighbors.

Several keen people have stepped forward recently hoping to 'solve' education. The founders' story typically goes along the lines of: 'I thought back to my own education, and I just knew that we could do it better.' Presumably in some respect education worked for these people since they are now in a position to start a company and raise millions of dollars in investment to try and make it work. As is always the case with startups, no matter what field they are in, doing it better means involving more technology.

Described a certain way, AltSchool, a San Francisco-based education startup begun in 2015, sounds like a nightmarish but unsubtly written near future dystopia - constant surveillance, never-ending performance measurement, learning metrics, tablet computers in front of eyeballs for hours a day. Its adherents see it as a way to provide a truly personalized learning experience for each child, letting them follow a line of study based on what they are actually interested in, instead of a class of children all being fed the same facts to memorize. Each classroom has a wide angle lens embedded in the wall which records everything that happens during the class for later analysis. The younger kids get all their information from tablet computers each is issued with. Anything a child creates is photographed and stored in their personal progress folder.

Helping educate children is one of the best things that tech people, so often viewed as rich, heartless robots, can do to be seen to be giving back to the world. AltSchool is a for-profit endeavor and every day fills up deep mines with data that can be extracted and sold later on. The school claims that it can collect data in a way which protects the anonymity of students, a ridiculous assertion given the low number of children enrolled since it has been shown to be possible to de-anonymize extremely large data sets with a high degree of accuracy using only a few points of reference.

Education and technology have a long and messy history together. After an inauspicious start, think of a lone BBC Micro or Archimedes computer and a similar number of staff who knew how to operate it, educators went for technology in a big way. It is not pleasant to think of the amount of money that has been handed over by educational boards over the last two decades for overpriced hardware and overhyped software, despite a slew of research calling into question the effectiveness of computer-based learning.

There is a popular movement right now in online education for adults, sites which aim to teach the actual day one skills that people who want to work in the tech industry will need. The platforms offering this education have partnered with some big names such as Google and have been able to slash the time needed to gain qualifications by only focusing on the practical skills employees need to hit the ground running. This came about as a result of too many computer science graduates entering the workplace after four years of solid study and lacking necessary competencies. AltSchool is also following this approach to an extent, claiming that they are teaching the skills needed so students can enter tomorrow's workplace.

Like blood in the water, the greater the amount of money involved, the more predators are drawn to the feeding frenzy. Mark Zuckerberg perhaps learned an expensive lesson a few years ago when $100m of his money was used in an ambitious effort to reform Newark's perpetually underperforming school system. The scheme was an almost complete failure, with much of the money going into the pockets of independent advisers. The local community actively rallied against the plans, arguing that they were sick of outside parties coming in and enforcing their ideas and beliefs on the local population, without engaging with that population at all. It was a complex and drawn out situation, sadly highlighting the dangers of assuming that funding alone is the cure.

Similarly, in 2010 Peter Thiel announced that he would pay college students $100,000 to drop out of their courses and instead focus on creating world-changing companies. Despite claiming to be frustrated with the quality of startups coming out of Silicon Valley, his largess seems to have funded a handful of familiar-sounding services, apps that pull info from other sources and yet more matchmaking systems.

People who have become disheartened with the whole environment complain about the lack of true innovation coming out of tech land. They point to the real nuts and bolts inventions that have had such transformative effects on the entire planet: mobile phones, jet engines, the microwave. The endless deluge of apps or services that just utilize the data flowing around the Internet don't stir the same kind of excitement and passion.

Perhaps we are expecting too much from the passengers of the Google buses, they are after all taking part in a gold rush so are naturally interested primarily in what the prospectors were: money.

No mention of Silicon Valley passes without a mention of the potential cash waiting to be grabbed by the next bright young thing. Crowdfunding capital, seed money, angel investment, B-round funding, stock options, IPOs. The people stepping off the train every week with a macbook tucked under their arm and keenness oozing from every pore are there to seek their fortune, not change the world; that's just the copy that gets sent out to the trade websites.

The smart ones have thought through the entire process, all the way through to the day when they can cash in their chips and jump ship. None of them wants to make a lifelong career out of managing an app that lets you rent out cats by the half-day and in this game, the longer that you stick with something, the greater the chance that it becomes suddenly obsolete. If you aren't one of the really big players, then your seat at the table is in no way assured and it is much better to try and judge when your service is at its peak popularity and get out, set a delay timer on the email so you can be away from the office before all the staff find out that the party is over.

Again the personal experiences of today's tech leaders are being used as justification for altering the system for everyone else. Both the current generation of industry CEOs and the one that came before them share certain similarities, the most obvious being intellect. Steve Jobs, Bill Gates, Mark Zuckerberg, Evan Williams (Twitter co-founder), Jan Koum (Whatsapp founder), Travis Kalanick (Uber founder) are all college dropouts. While the reasons varied, more than one seems to suggest that there was an element of frustration with the educational system. Quite likely, these people had been frustrated at the slow pace of school for some time.

It is little surprise then that today, many of them are advocates for student-centered learning, an educational philosophy popularized in the 50s and 60s by psychologist Carl Rogers. It rejects the traditional notion of a teacher delivering lecture-style lessons to rows of silent pupils and instead advocates pupils being given the means to essentially teach themselves.

They should be allowed to follow lines of enquiry based on what they find interesting and the teacher's job is to merely facilitate these opportunities. To anyone who sat through terms of lessons delivered by long-in-the-tooth teachers it sounds like paradise. It fits in neatly with the tech-utopian dream of classrooms full of kids armed with iPads conducting their own research into their chosen subject matter.

In late 2015 Facebook announced a joint venture with Summit Public Schools, a US-based network of charter schools, to create educational software. Specifically, this software would let students create tailored lessons and projects, with the teacher able to administer customized tests. Of course, the mere mention of Facebook and schools gets people understandably concerned about pupil privacy. Facebook claims that it doesn't collect any data from the Summit program, but as Google demonstrated, there's not collecting data and not collecting data.

Facebook aren't the only ones dipping their toe in to the education sector; plenty of startups are setting out to disrupt the classroom with new software and apps. In many cases, teachers are choosing themselves which services they want to try, leading to plenty of data leaks of students' information. That the teachers are able to do this is a result of the highly competitive nature of the market now, with hungry young companies directly pitching to classroom teachers, instead of the old route of going through the district educational board. The software tends to be offered under the freemium model, free for an individual teacher to use, but when that teacher tries to get the whole school on to it, then they have to pay to unlock extra features.

Educational boards are playing catchup, trying to get an understanding of just how many different products teachers are using and also the security and effectiveness of each. Teachers may not have a good understanding of what constitutes an acceptable data use policy when it comes to the personal information of the kids in their care. It isn't much of a stretch to imagine a company collecting data showing that a student is struggling in a particular area, then selling that information to the publishers of supplementary educational materials who happen to make a book on exactly what that child is having trouble with. In the United States at least, this direct-to-teacher marketing approach appears to violate some federal laws regarding pupil privacy.

Aside from the issue of how the software ends up in the classroom is the more important issue of whether it is any good or not. Truly independent research in this area is hard to come by, but for every study extolling the virtues of digital learning is another that concludes that it isn't any better and may be worse than traditional methods.

The National Education Policy Center, a research institute run out of the University of Colorado, conducted a study comparing traditional learning styles versus all digital and hybrid. They found that all-digital was no better and in some cases worse and that hybrid was in most cases no better, sometimes being more effective than traditional means, but the report noted that this came with a high price tag.

If teachers are being asked less to pass on their own knowledge and instead just manage a class of children who are conducting their own learning, then it seems possible that in the future, the requirement for the teachers to be highly educated in their chosen field may not be seen to be as important a factor.

Tech isn't just after the brains of today's students, however; it also wants their bodies. Dozens of perfectly normal, albeit grumpy-looking, children have been featured in newspapers holding up the letters they have received from their schools, informing them that they are dangerously obese according to the famously misleading BMI scale. Not satisfied with shaming kids into moving more, fitness trackers appear to be on the horizon for some students. Oral Roberts University requires that all students wear fitbit bracelets to ensure that they meet their minimum exercise requirements.

Although popular, the fitness trackers have a high rate of ending up in drawers next to old foreign currency and are as likely to make exercise a laborious chore as an enjoyable game. Critics have argued that college-age people are more prone to develop body image issues and that the mandated wearing of a fitness tracker will possible greatly exacerbate the problem of them becoming unhealthily preoccupied with their weight and fitness levels.

Since we remain among the first couple of generations to be exposed to these new technologies, we are the guinea pigs who will ultimately inform our successors of the long-term consequences of lives spent online. We don't have the data necessary to make conclusive statements regarding how useful technology is to education, for example. A worldwide experiment is currently underway as almost every school in the developed world has both invested heavily in IT equipment and made computing the center of the curriculum.

Critics worry than an over-reliance on using digital tools in the classroom leaves students unable to research information beyond googling it, and stifles independence of thought since all students are using the same sources of information. Some studies have dared suggest that students using pen and paper outperform those using laptops for taking notes when it comes to retaining the information later on. Given how essential parents are told digital skills are, nobody is clamoring for a return to chalk and blackboard.

2.12 Conclusion

In 2005, something akin to medieval times as far as the Internet is concerned, Alex Tew launched the million-dollar homepage, a maddeningly crude and effective way to generate money to pay off his student loans. A single webpage consisting of a 1000x1000 grid sold off to advertisers 100 pixels at a time, he earned $1,037,100 by the time the final pixel had been occupied, the last group of 1,000 being sold on eBay. The great-grandfather of modern crowdfunding, it attracted a lot of press attention as well as incredulity that it worked.

At that time, the online space was transitioning between a niche hobbyist pursuit and the all-encompassing behemoth it is today. By virtue of being first, the million-dollar homepage powerfully demonstrated that there was money to be made online. Facebook was still less than a year old at this point and only Google was really in the public consciousness.

11 years later and more happens online in a day than could ever be covered by the world's press or digested by its population. The Internet has the unique ability to be both maturing and constantly changing at the same time. Few people, however, are unaware of the knock-on effect that virtual actions have in the real world and that indeed, the line between the two is blurring as technology progresses.

Those who study the media landscape point out that television consumption is diminishing, the big screens in our living rooms losing the battle for our attention to the small screens of our tablets and smartphones. It is a mistake, however, to think of the Internet as just a modern television. TV is a strictly one-way affair, and the viewer is at all times just a consumer. Online, we can be creators, influencers, supporters or detractors. What happens there may be entertaining, but it is in no way just entertainment and those who realize the potential for what begins on a computer screen are those capable of upending the lives of everyone in the world.

The final part of this book has been set aside purely for the company which has essentially made all the others discussed here possible: Google. For a great many people Google is the Internet, the very strands of the World Wide Web, the building within which our visual notion of the Internet is housed.

Such is the size of the company, it is able to entertain and pursue ambitions beyond those of almost any other. That little rectangular box where you type search queries long ago became the least interesting or important thing about the company.

Google throws a lot of things at the wall, many slide harmlessly off, a few stick, and a few of those have the potential to change our lives in both subtle and overt ways.

3.1 Is that thing on? Google Glass lands

Announced in April of 2012 with the mission statement, 'We think technology should work for you — to be there when you need it and get out of your way when you don't.' Google Glass was one of the company's first big steps into the physical product realm. It quickly became a high-profile example of pushback against invasive technology.

Until Glass, the products which Google had made were fairly anonymous things like their Nexus handsets and Chromebooks. Products which arrived in a well-established market and could be viewed as pretty lazy attempts to quickly claim whatever share they could. Despite the popularity of the Android operating system, Google's own phone has never been a serious contender against the big names like Samsung and Apple and Chromebooks still struggle for mainstream acceptance.

Glass, however, was an entirely new product category, a consumer-level head-mounted display projecting information which seemed to hover in the wearer's field of vision. Launched in dramatic fashion in June 2012 during the I/O developer conference by a team of skydivers who were able to parachute on to the Moscone Center while livestreaming their descent, via Glass, to the audience who were watching inside, 2,000 pre-orders at $1,500 each were placed by people in order to become the first 'Google Glass Explorers'.

18 months and dozens of negative news reports later, the Glass program 'graduated' in what was commonly seen to be the quiet end of Google's aspirations of the product being a mass-market device.

Early adopters are a key factor in expensive, complicated technology being affordable for the general public. They serve not only to inject money into companies probably stretched by the financial burdens of production and marketing, but they are an early indication of the eventual popularity and viability of a product. It is one thing for a focus group to say they would pay x dollars for something, but it is another for them to actually hand over their own money.

In the case of the biggest tech companies, they do not need (as they occasionally demonstrate) to make a product which fulfils some kind of need in the marketplace, they can afford to produce and release practically anything and are easily able to absorb the cost of failure. Several moonshot projects have come from the once-famous but slightly misreported '20% time', the notion that Google employees are free to work on their own ideas for 20% of their working time (although they weren't the first; 3M had 15% time in the past).

Of course, these projects must be something which is going to be of benefit to Google. This strategy has been responsible for products such as Gmail, Google News and Adsense. Facebook has monthly Hackathons in which employees can work on their own ideas. The culture got a lot of attention and was seen for a time as a fundamental modern working practice for startups. Quite possibly it has also been behind some of the dozens of failed projects that these companies have generated over the years.

Although Google's 20% time was never formally adopted by the company, it was certainly well-documented for a time. Stories about the program started to taper off and recently it has been reported the the initiative is all but finished. Far from being a relaxed incubator of ideas, Google is a ruthlessly data-driven workplace. They are able to extremely accurately quantify, monitor and record the efficiency of each worker and team. This led to bosses being extremely reluctant to sign off on their subordinates' personal project time requests, as it would have a huge impact on the overall metrics for the entire team.

In the case of Google Glass, the lion's share of the blame for the terrible reception of the product has been put at the feet of the 'Explorers', the 2,000 pre-orders plus 8,000 winners of a contest for people who wrote 50 words or less on what they would do with the device. Attitude towards Glass quickly went from a 'what will they think of next' shrug to headlines proclaiming the end of privacy.

Google sought to conduct real-world testing by selling and giving away Glass; however, the target demographic was extremely narrow from the outset. The 2,000 developers, hardcore tech evangelists whose career or primary interest took them to the $900-a-ticket conference in San Francisco, an event for which Google randomly selected qualified attendees, those were not people with a passing interest in new technology.

The winners of the #ifihadglass contest certainly could have come from any walk of life, but in their initial advert for the promotion Google stated they were looking for 'bold, creative individuals'. Applicants could enter via Twitter or Google+ and could also include photos and videos. Couple this with the winners still having to pay $1,500 and it is easy to see why several news sources began claiming that Glass had a 'white, male' problem in terms of user diversity.

The $1,500 dollar price tag makes some interesting suggestions regarding Google's intentions for Glass. An initial report on the device by independent assessors claimed a parts price of $80, with the single most expensive component costing $14.

Of course, Google spent an unknown amount on R&D in terms of both money and manhours, but as occasionally the biggest publicly-traded company on the planet in terms of market cap, they could never be seen to be relying on the Glass Explorer program to generate profit for the company. Depending on how you like to do the math, Microsoft either makes $38.50 profit or a net loss on each Xbox sold, later recouping income from software sales and subscription purchases.

Instead, the $1,500 seems more like a barrier to entry, another way of weeding out people not onboard with their mission. They had been overtly exclusionary during stage one with the 2,000 developers by checking qualifications, and now they could do so again but more subtly by making it prohibitively expensive, more than double the price of the iphone 5 which was available at the same time. Users really had to love Google and the concept of Glass, and once they had $1,500 worth of tech on their face, then certainly their opinions and impression of it would be biased accordingly.

Before any of the Explorers even got their hands on Glass, however, the first official reaction to it was made when West Virginia proposed bill HB 3057, which included a ban on 'using a wearable computer with head mounted display' while driving. This was a perhaps slightly overzealous reaction to sensationalized stories which ignored the limitations of Google Glass and painted a picture of hundreds of motorists watching pornography while commuting to work. However, it would be the court of public opinion which would enact the greatest censure. One of the first announcements Google made which attempted to allay public fears was when they said that they would not approve any apps which used facial recognition, which unsurprisingly was a common fear for people when confronted by a camera that was potentially always looking at and recording them.

Once equipped, this small army of evangelists were sent out into the world to try and spread the word, and came away somewhat surprised by the generally frosty reception of public. Stories began to surface of wearers being verbally and physically assaulted for wearing the devices. These stories were typically met with a high level of anger towards the victim and further claims that they got what was coming to them.

Tech writer Robert Scoble dealt the device an early blow with a now-infamous photo of him wearing them while in the shower, claiming that he was never going to take them off. The picture did nothing to generate excitement for the device.

In large metropolitan areas, divisions quickly formed between the Explorers and the public. Many establishments sought to ban the wearing of the device on their premises and the Explorers fought back by leaving negative reviews of non-welcoming locations on sites like Yelp. These reviews of course frequently used the term 'luddite', suggesting that the people who had a problem with it either just didn't get it or were against new technology in general.

By the time the Explorers had been commonly redubbed 'Glassholes' and Google was having to publish advice on how not to be hated, it was difficult to see how the product was ever going to find traction or acceptance amongst the general public.

The problems with Glass likely began before the public was even aware of it. Reports from people who worked on it suggest an acknowledgment that the device wasn't ready and an impatient boss who would soon become caught up in an office romance with a Glass team employee which would lead to the end of his marriage. The reaction against the device, however, points not only to our own level of comfort with technology but also at the attitudes of the large tech companies.

Hundreds of new products are launched in this sector every year, both hits and misses, some are hated for not doing what they promised but few are seemingly purposefully drummed out of existence for doing (or perceived to be doing) what they were designed for. This is a gross division between the thinking of tech leaders and the people living in the world they are trying to hard to change.

Although Google went to great lengths to try and counter the notion, almost from launch the device was touted as a stalker's dream and most of the attention was directed at the camera pointed wherever the user looked. While Google attempted to make clear that the camera wasn't always on and would display a red light when recording, what the public saw was a nearly spy-sized recording device that was always aimed at them.

More than one Explorer had the headset physically torn from their face by irate people in bars and clubs. The product seemed to cross a societal boundary, doing nothing a smartphone already didn't but merely changing how the user interacted with it. By removing the act of taking the phone from the user's pocket, opening the camera app and overtly pointing the handset at what was being recorded, it changed the act to being somehow sneaky and creepy.

As well as the social factors, several physical ones also stood in the way of the device becoming a mainstream success. The official estimates from Google regarding battery life were about a day of normal use. Most reviews put it at more around the five-hour mark, and taking a video could wipe out the battery in as little as half an hour.

The point of Glass over a smartphone was that you would wear it all the time and it removed the need to take something out of your pocket to snap a photo. It was also immediately obvious when someone was wearing it, this probably being down to hardware size limitations over any thought to the social side. Because smartphone sizes are only getting bigger year after year, more research is going into the power contained within over the actual physical size, so currently the technology doesn't exist to shrink a battery down small enough while still providing a full days' worth of power.

It may be worth considering the first mobile phones; the very first models required a separate battery pack which the user wore slung over their shoulder. Very quickly the batteries got smaller and because the phone would only be used for the making and receiving of calls, the battery could happily last a few days or more between charges. Today's users have accepted the need to charge their devices at least daily and don't find this needlessly cumbersome given the amount they do on them.

When launched, the Apple Watch was widely derided for not really being able to tell the time for a full day if the user wanted to take advantage of all the features. It was seen as proof of the 'cult of Apple' that they could sell a timepiece for as much as $17,000 for the top of the line model which wouldn't see you from midnight Monday all the way to midnight Tuesday.

Importantly, the physical problems are only temporary. Batteries will continue to get smaller and more powerful and if Google or another company are able to incorporate the display of the device into the lenses of the glasses without anything protruding, then they will have overcome the major hurdle: stigma. However, they should look at the relatively lukewarm reception that smartwatches have received as an indicator of how much people want an always-present device, even heavy users of smartphones.

It would seem that people are happy to take the device out of their pocket when they want to use it and put it away again when they are done. It is obviously more convenient to glance at a watchface yet many see the Apple Watch as the company's first modern-era failure. It may be that for most of the public, there is little desire to be visually assaulted with information all day long.

Google Glass seems to be less an attempt to fill a gap in the market and more just Sergey Brin acting out his Tony Stark fantasies at the expense of the comfort of everyone else. A blindness or arrogance about the role of personal technology and how far people are prepared to accommodate it and also an exclusionary feeling of 'them' and 'us', either being completely for technology or against it, with no middle ground.

John Hanke, CEO of Niantic, makers of Pokemon Go, originally envisioned players of their massively popular game wearing Internet-connected contact lenses to see the characters they were hunting for, instead of using their smartphones. Microsoft released in augmented reality headset in 2016. It seems likely that the evolution and miniaturization of this technology will continue, with Glass being a mere temporary setback.

Glass has been put to fantastic use in a very narrow range of situations, most notably by allowing surgeons to record and stream a first-person view of surgical procedures. This is undeniably a wonderful learning tool so it makes sense that the Glass team is now intending the product to be used primary as an aid to skilled labor. Several competing models have sprung up, all looking and behaving broadly similar to Glass, with Sony being the biggest name involved.

3.2 Look both ways: self-driving cars are coming for you

Coming soon to a street near you, a car that, as it sees you, will judge your worth as a human being and whether or not you deserve to live should it need to kill somebody.

Tech companies hate people. We are slow, irrational and often need to go to the toilet. They have decided that people are the problem with everything and that computers, the same ones that throw up weird error messages on your screen and for no reason fall out with the printer that they were previously friends with, should run everything. What better place to start than with driving, one of the least consequence-free human activities?

Google of course are at the forefront of this. Their cute little cars have been trundling around roads in California for five years now, not killing anyone, pulling over for the police and generally doing a great job of driving. The first noteworthy collision occurred in January 2016 when both the car and a human bus driver made assumptions about what the other would do and the two struck each other, thankfully only at 2mph. More worryingly, Google seems to be feeling rather impatient with the progress of getting these cars out onto the open road.

In March 2016 Chris Urmson, principal engineer on Google's self-driving car project, sent a letter to the US Transportation Secretary arguing that driverless cars should be road-legal if they can pass a standardized federal safety test. Crucially, Google distrust humans so much that they want to completely do away with both the steering wheel and pedals in order to remove the chance of an illogical, emotional person suddenly trying to wrest control back from the computer.

As is common when dealing with technology or services which have an impact on an established way of doing things, the government is rushing to catch up with market maker's ambitions. All current regulations were written with soft, irreplaceable humans in mind and so obviously would need to be reworked for loveless robot drivers. The risk is that because both UK and US governments are now on the back foot, responding to pressure from huge companies who are eager to put a price tag on these inventions and get them in showrooms, there is a strong chance that policy may be dictated to them and the needs and wants of the road-interacting public could be given slightly less attention.

The National Highway Traffic Safety Administration (NHTSA) is rushing to get a set of guidelines out the door in order to try and get the growing number of parties developing autonomous vehicles on the same page. Actual fixed regulations can take years to be finalized so the guidelines are seen as a stopgap measure. Some automakers fear that with the tail wagging the dog, the guidelines may prove inadequate. The NHTSA countered that they have little choice, since driverless cars are being unleashed on to public roads in various forms whether they like it or not. Many of the most pessimistic believe that it will take the first death to result in meaningful action being taken to address the reality that several companies are turning public roads into test tracks while they try to iron out all the kinks in the code.

Tech companies are very skilled at dressing up their reasons for wanting to dominate a market and earn billions of dollars. Uber wants to help African-Americans get around and make female passengers feel safe getting home from a night out. Google wants to reduce road deaths and help people with mobility issues. These goals prevent good amounts of criticism towards the company's other practices from being voiced.

The self-driving car concept was announced by Google in 2011. Since then, the time frame for when we'd all have to start worrying about cutting off a Terminator on the motorway has changed over time from anywhere between five and 30 years. It seems that Google rather oversold how close they were to completing this project initially and a good amount of observers now believe that the days of people steering and braking their own cars aren't yet severely limited. We're all aware of the promises made regarding technology and what they actually deliver; we should be living in moon base houses by now using personal jet packs to get around. There is always the feeling that this time it's different when it comes to what's around the corner. The mere possibility that self-driving cars might appear on the roads within the next one to two decades is having real, observable consequences right now to the millions and people who currently use public transport.

In 2014, a proposal to overhaul the public transport in Pinellas County, Tampa Bay failed at a public vote. The plan was to expand the city's bus service and construct a new light rail system. Construction would have been paid for by an increase in sales tax. The Tampa Bay region is consistently ranked extremely poorly in transportation and livability indexes, with long commuting times and poor pedestrian facilities. Before the vote, Florida State Senator Jeff Brandes argued against the plans, claiming that the entire debate over investment in public infrastructure was moot given that in 15 to 20 years everyone would be zipping around in personal transportation pods. It is impossible to say how much effect his opinion had on the overall outcome of the vote, but it is dispiriting to see public officials willing to make people continue to suffer today because things might get better in the future.

This new technology is being touted as universal transport for all, one of the ways that it is threatening investment in current public transport infrastructure. Right now, the cars are being tested on the beautiful, driver-friendly mountain roads in California. The cars do very well there, it is sunny and bright much of the time and compared to places like congested city centers and motorways, the drive is comparatively easy. Quite likely, this will be the first market that the cars are available to, affluent Bay-Area first adopters.

It is impossible to predict the final effect that the emergence of autonomous cars will have on the auto industry. It is naive to think that things will remain exactly as they were before, except we'll all be sat in the driver's seat reading newspapers while we commute. The entire concept of car ownership is being put at risk by groups who want the computer cars to zip around all day, taking people from A to B on demand. For people who have seen the opportunities to create middlemen where none existed before this is an exciting concept. Right now, once the car is paid for the customers relationship with the manufacturer is largely over. The only ongoing costs are tax, insurance, fuel and repairs. If the ambition is made real and automakers succeed in innovating themselves out of a job, it would have a transformative effect on the world exactly equal but perhaps opposite to the release of the Ford Model T.

To truly appreciate what is at stake for the auto industry, it is important to consider the almost impossible complexity of how modern cars are produced. Take one model of car, and specifically one part of that car. A Japanese company called Tokai Rika produces seatbelts and some of the plastic switches used in the steering column. They produce parts for several manufacturers but mainly Toyota. The company is over 70 years old, employs over 16,000 people and has factories in countries around the world.

The parts that it produces are made from materials and components purchased from other companies further down the supply chain. The mass of materials and components are shipped from the supplier to Tokai Rika several times a day through the famous 'just-in-time' system of trucks continually delivering parts as they are needed for production.

The finished parts are likewise sent on to Toyota. The 16,000 employees work in R&D, design, production, sales, HR and all the other departments a typical company has. Many of the full time staff can expect to work there for their entire careers and may have joined the company straight from university. A huge, complex company in its own right, reliant on other equally large companies, all to just make the seatbelt and the window wiper control stick. Multiply this by the thousands of other parts in a car, produced by hundreds of different companies, all with history of their own. When considering the sheer amount of people and effort needed to produce the parts for one car, it is amazing that it can be sold so cheaply yet support so many.

If this were eventually to stop and consumers only had a choice between summoning either a shared Google car or a shared Apple car to take them to their destination, it would have possibly involved the destruction of millions of jobs. In the same way that the automobile changed the very structure of the country, moving many who could afford it into the suburbs, there would be another radical shift in the makeup of urban geography and where people choose to live. Every other so-called innovation or advancement brought on by the tech industry in recent times has led to fewer jobs in real terms and more money going to fewer people.

Rather than suddenly replacing all drivers with autonomous vehicles, what we will more likely see is gradually more and more control given over to the car. Already many models feature things such as automatic braking. In 2016, Tesla beamed out an over-the-air update to its 2014 and later models which enabled an autopilot feature. Owners suddenly found their vehicles able to not only maintain speed but also position as well thanks to the autosteer feature. The car utilized its onboard cameras and GPS sensors to keep the car in lane, even when going round bends. The cars were also now capable of changing lanes in response to the driver using the turn signal. The cars could parallel park on their own and reverse out of the garage without the owner being in the vehicle.

Around two months after the update, changes were made to the autosteer feature after it became obvious that drivers were ignoring the warnings that it was not a fully autonomous feature and that they needed to remain largely in control of the vehicle at all times. Several videos were posted showing the cars traveling at high speeds with the driver not holding the wheel or in some cases not even being in the driver's seat.

Aside from people just playing with the system, more than one video surfaced which seemed to show drivers having to suddenly take control in order to save themselves from a possible collision caused by the car making dangerous maneuvers of its own accord, such as veering into the oncoming traffic lane.

Other than the warning to be careful, little guidance was given by the company on the use of the technology. Indeed, it was released as a public beta, meaning that it wasn't in a final state yet and that the drivers using it would be test pilots. This is fine for the car owners, who have been given a choice in the matter, but every other road user has had that choice taken away from them, since they are now forced to share the road with a car capable in a definite respect of driving itself but which is running on software the makers say is not fully ready. It is a mistake to think that it is brave Tesla early-adopters who are testing this system; it is all of us, whether we like it or not.

If a collision were to occur, Tesla claims that it would always be the driver who is liable, although just making that statement doesn't automatically protect them from legal action. Tesla says that the system will get better as more people use it and data is fed back to them. It is difficult to think of many other products released as unsafe but with the claim that they will be made safer over time.

Thanks to emissions targets introduced under the Obama administration, Tesla has been the benefactor of hundreds of millions of dollars' worth of environmental credits. Emissions targets are calculated on a manufacturer's entire output, not on a car-by-car basis. This encourages auto makers to keep investing in and producing electric and hybrid vehicles even as sales rates remain extremely low. If the manufacturers can't meet the emissions targets, they can pay a fine or buy a credit. Because Tesla's entire fleet is electric, they are given these credits by the government for effortlessly hitting the targets. Tesla can then sell these credits to other car makers who can use them to pay off the government if their fleet doesn't meet the target, they don't produce any electric/hybrid cars or they want to intentionally limit the amount of these kind of cars that they produce. As you can imagine, Tesla is pushing hard to try and make these emissions targets tougher. Publicly because of the environmental impact of petrol and diesel engines, but privately for the millions in extra dollars it will bring to the company.

The quite incredible capability that Tesla has to reach out to all its cars and make dramatic changes by altering the software is what allows it such a huge amount of freedom when it comes to regulations. The regulatory bodies, who have had to concern themselves only with the nuts and bolts level of cars since their inception, are now living in a world where software has become absolutely vital to the operation of the car. The NHTSA currently lumps software with other non-essential car components like the entertainment system.

On May 7th 2016, Joshua Brown unfortunately became something of a person of note when he became the first person to be killed while in the driver's seat of a vehicle driving itself, in this case a Tesla Model S. Several early and contradictory reports claimed things like he was watching a movie at the time of the crash. A report by the National Transportation Safety Board said that the vehicle, which was in self-drive mode, was speeding. It is believed that a truck towing a large white trailer pulled out in front of the Tesla, which failed to detect the white trailer against the background of the bright sky.

Of all the major manufacturers who are working on self-driving technology, only Tesla is testing their system on the open road. It is perhaps no coincidence that they are also the youngest company, the others having spent the last few decades of their existence keenly aware of the overriding importance of safety in the minds of the consumer when choosing which car to buy.

It is unrealistic to put a driver behind the wheel of a car capable of maintaining speed, distance from other vehicles and position on the road then expect the driver to be ready to take over at a moment's notice should the system fail. Google believes that humans can't take control and correct a situation quickly enough, which is why they want to have no human-operable controls in their cars whatsoever. As soon as people have the option of the car doing some of the work, naturally they want to take advantage of it. Tesla cars require that the drivers touch the steering wheel every few seconds so that the car knows they are still paying attention. Other manufacturers' systems require the driver's hands to be on the wheel at all times.

The recently announced Self-Driving Coalition for Safer Streets promises to give government regulators headaches as they begin a big push for autonomous vehicles. The group, comprised of Google, Lyft, Uber, Ford and Volvo and headed by a former administrator of the NHTSA, David Strickland, aims to get self-driving cars on the roads as soon as possible.

Both Lyft and Uber want the same thing in this case: human drivers away from the wheel, and consequently away from the courthouse talking to judges about whether they are employees or not. Their motivations have nothing to do with a desire for safer streets and more to do with eliminating their current biggest outgoing, driver recompense. Given that the vast majority of auto accidents are caused by some form of driver error, it remains unclear exactly why the coalition is seemingly so concerned with safer streets, since the automobile manufacturers aren't being blamed for people texting and driving. Quite probably 'safer streets' just has a nicer ring to it than the Self-Driving Coalition for Making Money and Putting People out of Work.

Although the coalition hasn't done anything concrete yet, it seems likely to many that one of the aims of the lobbying group will be to attempt to insulate both hardware and software makers from responsibility arising from the inevitable accidents which are going to occur when we see a mass rollout of this kind of cars.

Giving the car eyes, whether that be high definition cameras, radar sensors or network connectivity is already well within the manufacturers' capabilities. Having the car steer and operate itself is similarly possible. The challenge is going to be in the code, the millions of lines of it needed to allow the computer to take all the collected sensory information it is being fed and make sense of it at 70mph. Code is written by people, people make mistakes, code is perpetually being exploited and repaired, cracked and fixed, updated, improved and unintentionally spoiled. It's nothing more than a frustration when it comes to the computer sat on your desk, it is something else altogether when it's in the car carrying you and your family.

A collision is coming, that is without doubt, and this one is going to be between regulators and those who have made large investments in the technology which underpins the concept of driverless cars. The people who have large financial stakes in this aren't going to like the idea of being told that it is 40 years away from being on the road, and therefore being profitable. If the regulators are seen to be slowing the pace of innovation then the lobbyists will start billing lots of overtime hours.

This has been demonstrated most recently by the reaction of Google to the news that draft rules from California's Department of Motor Vehicles stipulate that a human driver must be present in the vehicle at all times. It is Google's ambition that not only should a driver not be needed, but that he or she should lack the ability to take control of the vehicle even if desired, since there would be no steering wheel or pedals. It was forced to include the controls to ensure the legality of the cars when they hit public roads. The tech giant said that it was 'gravely disappointed' at the draft legislation and hinted that the DMV was trying to stop us all living in a Jetsons-style technological paradise. The legislation also made clear that in the event of a collision, the human would be held liable, not the car. Google, along with Volvo and Mercedes-Benz, had already stated that they would accept liability if their vehicles caused an accident.

In California, 11 auto makers are permitted to test autonomous vehicles. All will have different and competing software and hardware systems, and naturally some will be smarter and safer than others. Will the manufacturers of the stupidest robot driver's license the technology from someone who's done it better, or will consumers be able to buy a driverless car for less money but on the understanding that their chauffeur is a few circuits short of a motherboard?

Tech companies would do well to learn from the successes that companies such as Uber have had at building public support for something by quickly making it common and plainly useful, which then prevented regulators attempts to reign in the company. If the people who desire to ultimately sell a driverless car in showrooms across the country can get sufficient numbers of passengers into safe, comfortable pre-programmed rides in and out of the city which let them work, read or watch a movie while they travel, then these same people are going to support efforts to get the cars rolled out onto every road as soon as possible.

Self-driving cars are already being tested in some cities, although they are much more modest in their capabilities. These vehicles just follow a predetermined route and simply brake if they detect something that they don't like. Their decision making capabilities are severely limited. This is seen as a good way not only to test the technology and improve on it, but also to gently get the public used to the idea of seeing cars pass them by with completely empty front seats, not just carrying small elderly people.

Because the success of the self-driving care relies on it so much, the topic of these autonomous vehicles is closely linked with the discussion on the future of artificial intelligence. As AI gets smarter and better able to learn with every passing day, experts in the field are starting to have serious talks about how best humankind should approach the difficult subject of there quite possibly being on Earth someday an entity greatly more intelligent than the ones who created it. The people taking this concept seriously fall either into 'full steam ahead' or 'hold on a second'.

The most high profile people advocating caution are Professor Stephen Hawking and worryingly, Elon Musk, who in 2015 donated $10m to the Future of Life Institute to help ensure that nobody built a computer called Skynet that could start a nuclear war. This money was seen as a welcome boost to the study of the implications of the technology, instead of money for the technology itself which had always been the main beneficiary of funding. It also helped start many of the conversations and debates on what role AI should play in people's lives if and when it ever became advanced enough.

For his trouble, Elon Musk, who is in all but name Tony Stark, was nominated as one of the Information Technology & Innovation Foundation's (ITIF) Luddites of the Year. The think-tank published a list of 10 nominees who all stood accused of standing in the way of innovation and generally just spoiling everyone's fun by whining on about safety and ethics. Also on their list was anywhere that had sided with taxi drivers over ride-sharing companies, the Center for Food Safety for opposing genetically modified food and advocates seeking to ban killer robots.

The ITIF holds the same tired opinion that most do when they find their endeavors halted, however briefly, by people or organizations voicing concerns. They label the opposition as neo-luddites. This generalization implies anyone who is at all concerned by the rapid advances of technology and who wishes for any kind of legal or ethical framework to be put in place is someone who is against all innovation and wants the human race to go back to tilling the land with a horse-drawn plow and spending evenings reading by candlelight.

Not long after the first reports of driverless cars being let loose on the roads came the first stories of these cars being hacked. The attacks ranged from making the cars see objects around them that weren't really present, thereby instigating some kind of evasive action, all the way to taking full control of the vehicle from a distance.

Although hackers will continue to pose a risk to the safety of people using the vehicles (and people around them), the barrier to entry for people wanting to attack a robot car is still quite high. They must be personally present near their target and have the physical tools necessary. Importantly, there is currently no financial incentive for people to carry out such attacks and until there is, the numbers will be confined to people who just want to do it for malicious reasons. 75% of new cars will feature some sort of online connectivity by 2020.

Regardless of your own feelings towards driverless cars, if you are a road user then you may find yourself directly affected anyway. One of the biggest problems that the autonomous cars have is trying to predict and account for what human drivers are likely to do. A group of computer cars traveling near each other can easily talk to one another directly and can know exactly what each individual vehicle is doing and wants to do. Human drivers have to interpret a complex set of signals, some of them subconscious. The only information we are directly presented with are the brake and turn lights, not much of a clue really, since the turn lights can be used accidentally or not at all. To aid us, we take into account the driving style of the other car, its size (and reputation) and we also make judgments if we are able to see if the driver is old or young, male or female, etc. This is a considerable challenge for a computer.

If all cars were replaced by autonomous computer drivers tomorrow, things would be very easy. Barring outside interference, there would be no more traffic jams, no road rage. The problem will be the mix of human and non-human drivers. Computers will have a hard time reading us and vice versa. A group of researchers at MIT demonstrated a model in March 2016 which showed that when the roads are populated entirely by computer controlled cars, there won't be any need for traffic lights at junctions, since the cars can communicate so well with each other, they can decide in a fraction of a second who will go and who will yield. The result is a scary-looking but very efficient flow of traffic.

Do you think that, when these cars are on the roads and have gained widespread adoption, human drivers are going to be allowed to carry on as usual? We will still need stop lights, which will slow the whole process down and entirely negate the advantages of the computer cars' communication system, since they will all be sitting around knowing exactly what everyone is going to do but waiting to see what this crazy person waiting at the light might decide on. Go right, go left, get out of the car and defecate in the middle of the crossing? All are possible when it comes to people.

It would be nice to think that industry and government will wait until the last real driver hands over his license sometime in 2080, but obviously this is not going to happen.

Collisions are much more likely to occur between people and computers, and people and people, rather than computers and computers. When figures are published demonstrating this it will lend weight to the calls to get humans out of the driver's seat once and for all.

When suddenly confronted with the possibility of a major collision happening at high speed, humans don't have time to consciously weigh up all the possible outcomes of their actions in order to choose the best course. They act instinctively and this instinct is guided in part by the total accumulation of the beliefs and prejudices they have formed over their lifetime. This may manifest itself as either self-preservation, self- sacrifice or trying to ensure the survival of passengers in the car. Often there is seemingly no logical outcome to such a terrible event. Computers only operate on one level and do nothing on instinct. They will have more time to assess a situation, assigning metrics to all the players taking part in this little slice of drama and then making decisions based on each character's perceived value.

Self-driving technology is slowly creeping into today's vehicles. Many new models feature some sort of auto-stop system, which can apply the brakes without human intervention if the car detects some kind of obstruction in front. Usually this system works at slow speeds, under 17kph and the car doesn't have to worry about the implications for other drivers as anyone traveling behind is always expected to maintain a safe distance between themselves and the car in front. The cars don't care what the obstruction is, which is good news for small animals who may otherwise find themselves not ranked that highly on the importance chart.

Although they have benefited from a large amount of positive press coverage, the truly driverless car may be further away than people like to admit. Driving involves utilizing such a complex set of skills that it may take technology decades to fully emulate them. The physical act of controlling the steering and pedals is the least of the engineers' concerns. Drivers have to visually detect, recognize, interpret and process every single object which they encounter during the journey. Computers still struggle with reliably identifying objects; even scores of 95% accuracy are nowhere near enough.

Humans also have to know the nature of the objects, not just categorize them. They have to know that a three-year-old walking down the street with their parent is more likely to suddenly dart into the road than an 8-year-old. They can recognize the tell-tale sign of an seemingly empty driver's seat in the car in front and assume that it's one of the fleet of elderly drivers who seem to barely be able to see over the steering wheel, and so change their driving style in response. Even socio-economic factors play a part, rightly or wrongly. A driver going through a less affluent housing estate may subconsciously be aware of the possibility of groups of unattended children allowed to roam free, even if this is not the case.

The number of deaths occurring on U.S. roads annually is just over 32,000, down for a high of over 43,000 in 2003. The leading causes of these accidents are distracted driving, speeding, drunk driving and reckless driving. The fifth leading cause is rain, over which we have no control. It doesn't make a great case for having people behind the wheel that the top four causes of death on the roads are all our own fault. Drivers are assaulted with distractions when operating modern cars. 20 years ago all they had to fiddle with was the radio and an ineffective heater. Now mobile phones, increasingly complex center consoles, sat-nav systems and in-car entertainment all combine to keep drivers' attention off the road in front. Laws have been passed which attempt to curtail the use of mobile phones whilst driving but many drivers continue to do so, led by a powerful combination of factors, belief that they are safer and better drivers than others and programmed behavior which makes it difficult to ignore an incoming phone call.

Given that bad driving is the cause of so many deaths on the road, there are those that believe that it is unethical to needlessly delay the introduction of more sophisticated computer-controlled cars, since any kind of reduction in fatalities would be worth it.

The public is going to wrongly expect computer-controlled cars to be perfect, and will be disproportionately outraged when the first major incidents start to occur.

In some auto accidents, there may be no way for the computer, who is a slave to the physics of the situation, to entirely avoid contact with a vehicle or person, but that will be a tough sell to people caught up in grief and shock. A consortium of AI experts rightly said 'If self-driving cars cut the roughly 40,000 annual US traffic fatalities in half, the car makers might get not 20,000 thank-you notes, but 20,000 lawsuits.'

3.3 Hedges vs tech: Google streetview comes to every town

Google started big and bold when they began doing things in the real world without request or permission. In 2007, off the back of the Standford CityBlock Project, they went out into the world and photographed it, practically all of it (as far as areas inhabited by humans are concerned). They drove down five million miles of road, snapping 9 photos every 10-20 meters (satellite photos range from 15 meters to 15 centimeters in resolution). Where the roads weren't suitable for cars, they rode specially adapted bikes. When they couldn't use the bikes they strapped the apparatus to people's backs and shoved them out the door.

They now have over 20 petabytes of data which is updated as often as possible. It makes the oft-maligned government services like the NSA look like someone using a glass against the wall to listen to a conversation in the next room, but it's certainly fun to see where you live on the computer isn't it?

Their mission statement is to 'organize the world's information and make it accessible and useful'. Really it should also contain the words 'gather', 'collect' or 'harvest' since they are busy extracting this information, not just organizing it.

Despite American's vocal hatred of their domestic security services, they have never lived under overt surveillance. Germany, one of the most privacy-focused countries on the planet, has a long and complicated history of monitoring its inhabitants. It acted quickly to stop Google from mapping any more of its streets. Not prevent, stop. Google didn't explicitly ask permission from many countries it entered, it just started doing so. The reason for this is that data, unlike any other commodity, cannot be handed back.

If Shell had taken oil from somewhere without drilling rights, either that physical oil could be returned, an equal amount of oil, or money equaling the amount taken. Data is Google's forever since it is impossible to verify whether or not it has been deleted. That it why it is important to adopt a 'seek forgiveness, not permission' attitude.

In the face of mounting concern about the ramifications of this practice when it became public knowledge, Google said that individuals could opt out and have their residences blurred from view. This shifted the onus to act off Google and onto, well everyone else living on the planet. It was now up to them to know what Google had done, know they had a choice and finally be in a position to contact Google, something which had to be done online.

Because the data they collect can be easy copied and distributed, usually without severely impacting the value of the original information, Google can share much of what it collected during the Streetview program and make it accessible to anyone for free. This is the key factor in separating something which would be seen as horribly intrusive and terrifying, a black car with CIA stickers on the door, driving slowly down your street taking photos every few feet, and something benevolent and useful, a brightly colored Google car doing the same thing, only they are going to share the information with you. Regardless of what else they do with the data, the public's interaction is with a service, and an extremely useful one at that.

And because, if you are going to go to the trouble of sending cars down every street on the planet, you might as well make the most of it, Google also decided to hoover up vast amounts of information from unencrypted Wi-Fi routers in every home and building they drove past.

Google adopted a three-stage approach to this story. First they tried denying that it was taking place, then they claimed that in certain cases very small fragments of data packets had been collected, finally they admitted that entire communications, including email addresses and passwords, had been gathered. They eventually dropped the notion that the data had been collected accidentally, instead finally admitting to the Federal Communications Commission (FCC) that the data collection was the result of a deliberate decision by a member of Google's staff working on the Streetview project.

The engineer in question exercised his Constitutional right not to testify. Partially as a result of this, significant technical questions relating to the Wi-Fi snooping couldn't be answered, and the FCC could not press ahead with charges under Section 705(a) of the 1934 Communications Act.

By gathering the data and then taking their chances in court, what Google essentially did was to just purchase the information. They would have been well aware of the theoretical maximum liabilities that they would have faced in the event of successful court action against them.

They also have the legal resources to keep these things in the courts for years at a time. If they win then that's fine, if they eventually lose they still retain the collected data. In March 2011, France's Commission Nationale de l'Informatique et des Libertés (CNIL) fined Google €100,000 for violating French privacy laws. Two months later, the Department of Justice closed its own investigation, deciding not to seek charges against the company. The CNIL fine was just under three minutes' worth of profit for Google. You win some, you win some.

The UK's Information Commissioner's Office (ICO) received communication from Google in 2012 that it had found remnants of materials it had been ordered to destroy back in 2010. In the same year the FCC issued Google with an Apparent Liability of Forfeiture for ignoring five requests for a signed declaration to the accuracy of the FCC's Letter of Inquiry.

In the cases where Google has been found liable and ordered to hand over money, the amounts involved have been a drop in the ocean for a company Google's size. This is due to the age and unsuitability of the laws of which the company has fallen foul. Most were created to cover technologies like radio and telephone communications. Since this case was tried, in 2012 the General Data Protection Regulation was created in the EU to replace the aging laws. Under it, fines of up to €20m or 4% of the worldwide annual turnover (whichever is greater) of the offending company can be issued. This act also includes the well-publicized 'right to be forgotten' policy, which allows people to request that search engines remove links to websites about them.

The Streetview project met with resistance in several countries. In Japan, the imagery collected initially showed people's faces, car registration plates and also the family name plates which are attached to some residential buildings. After concerns were raised over the privacy implications, Google Japan agreed to contact local governments in future. Amazingly, they stated that they had sought the approval of governments in other some countries, but had not done so in Japan because they were unaware of the potential privacy concerns.

It is obvious that Google greatly increased the success of the Streetview project by adopting this approach of beginning without proper consultation, then letting citizens and governments do the job of rushing around and trying to ascertain what information was being gathered and how it was being used. It is a lot simpler for a government to deny a request to do something than it is to try and stop something already in progress. By getting the information into public hands as soon as possible, they were able to present users with an undeniably useful tool which would distract them from the incredible liberties that had been taken with their freedom.

Despite the camera cars being unwelcome in several countries, there is still enough of the world left to map to keep Google busy. As they add more and better imagery of the places they can go, the residents of off-limits areas may begin to feel left out rather than protected. Several places which halted the progress of the project still display imagery taken before the injunction, but now it is out of date and seems to point to a backwards or regressive policy rather than a privacy-minded one.

Although Google is a huge company, in terms of the number of users vs. employees, it has to take advantage of the leverage that the Internet affords in letting a relatively small group of people be able to service many millions of customers. So the burden is very much placed on the user to do anything. Streetview was briefly banned in Austria before being allowed under the proviso that citizens could request to have their properties blurred out. Because this requires a human to manually carry out this task, it proved too much of a problem for Google, who just suspended the project altogether, as it had in Germany under similar circumstances.

During the early days of the project when there was lots of news coverage of it, one concern was of the potential benefit to terrorists of having such detailed maps of places they intended to attack. While there has been anecdotal evidence that terrorists have used Google Earth and Streetview, it is only another source of intelligence for them and certainly can't be held responsible as the deciding factor between an attack being carried out or not. Depending on the location, imagery can several years old and is not updated frequently enough to be of real use to people who require absolutely accurate information about what is on the ground.

To take advantage of the average Internet user's propensity for sharing, Google now uses imagery taken by any member of the public. People are encouraged to use their smartphones, DSLR cameras or even special cameras which are designed to take a 360-degree spherical photo of a scene to photograph and upload images of anywhere they want. By involving people in this way Google cuts the effort needed to maintain imagery of popular places to nearly zero, and it also makes the public a part of this project and therefore much less likely to complain about it.

If you have ever signed up for a new online service or attempted to login to a site and been presented with a strangely garbled but just about readable set of numbers and letters, you've seen a captcha, a method of differentiating between computer and people and the primary way of stopping automated software from creating fake accounts on websites. Sometimes instead of the generated characters, you may have seen what looks like a cropped photo of a house number. This is Google using people to help enter data into their Streetview project on their behalf.

Because computers are quite bad at this job compared to people, they decided to have people (more often than not unwittingly) contribute to the program and to make it more accurate. Millions of people are presented with these images taken from the photos of people's houses and they duly type in the numbers they see. There is a good chance that you have also helped Google with their effort to digitize every book in existence, as words generated from this scheme are also presented for human verification.

Streetview has weathered the storm. It is no longer something which is marveled over or discussed and has gone from potentially creepy intrusion to just another thing that exists online. Now that they've outsourced the maintenance to an army of volunteers (who are rewarded with free space on Google Drive or the eligibility to apply to attend a tour of the Google campus) they can keep the service current. No other organization would ever dream of repeating the feat and as each day passes, the question of the privacy of the people who have been photographed becomes less of an issue.

Despite humanity's claimed fear of mass surveillance, the foundations are being laid, and against very few people's will. By involving people in the efforts and making something which can be an extremely useful if little-considered service, it becomes an accepted part of life. Glass was a step too far, a literally in-your-face attempt at information gathering. Streetview is fast becoming an essential utility.

3.4 Page turners: Google swallows the library

We can see parallels between the Streetview project and Google Books, the effort by the company to eventually scan all printed books in existence and make them available online. This endeavor is another example of the way in which the idea of democratization of information can be used to sidestep what would, in most normal circumstances, be a fairly open and closed case of copyright infringement.

While Streetview drove down the world's roads, sucking up all the visible and invisible information it could, the book project sauntered down the library aisles, indiscriminately digitizing everything it could get its hand on. Authors and publishers were taken aback by the intrusion on their turf. Unless a book had already been released digitally, it was somewhat safe from piracy since nobody was going to take the time to sit and type up the whole thing, and even scanning it at home was an incredibly laborious process. Suddenly the specially-designed apparatus of the book project was gobbling up tomes at a rate of 1,000 pages an hour and spewing the results online. Lawsuits arrived like mosquitoes at a BBQ. They were gathered together for the sake of simplicity then quickly beaten in the court.

The book project is really what Google was all about before it became Google. Co-founders Sergey Brin and Larry Page came up with the idea of digitizing library books and then using the amount of citations between volumes as an indicator of the book's usefulness and relevance. This concept was then applied to the information available online and the rest became profitable history.

The company didn't singlehandedly come up with the concept of scanning huge amounts of printed information. Libraries around the world had been struggling with the idea for some time as a way of preserving their massive collections but were severely limited by the comparatively scant resources available to them. Google was able to come up with a non-destructive method which worked quickly enough to make the ultimate aim of scanning every single printed book in existence feasible.

In the early days of the project, there seemed to be little effort made at filtering what was and wasn't to be included. The books chosen were a mix of public domain, copyright but out of print and copyright and in print. In fact, out of these three categories, public domain works made up the least initially, with the in copyright but out of print (orphaned as Google referred to them) making up the bulk.
Google claimed that they had been unable to contact the owners of these orphaned works but it is debatable how much time the company spent trying to reach over five million authors. In the early days, Google's policy regarding copyright books was to scan it unless the author asked them not to, the tried and trusted method of shifting the burden away from themselves and on to others.

Interestingly, the project faced criticism from two sources: the first were the authors and publishers who rightly feared loss of profits, the second was from academics who had hoped to make use of the service. Their complaint was that the great majority of the scanned work was so riddled with errors as to render the final product useless, unreadable. The imposing-looking book scanner was capable of extremely high speeds, but the bottleneck in the process was always going to be checking what was produced. That needed human eyes working at painfully slow human speed. The books were therefore never checked and released as is. The Optical Character Recognition (OCR) software which converted the images into searchable text obviously wasn't 100% accurate, making searching and reading the text a frustrating process. The scheme also came under fire for the amount of English language work scanned compared to other languages, something critics feared might adversely shape future research.

The notion of scanning rare books makes perfect sense. Some of the most revered works in our shared literary history may exist, in their original form, as only a handful of physical copies, accessible to only trusted scholars. The preservation of aging creative work is a pressing problem. As with other projects which are founded under noble ideals, the scope quickly changed and grew until the original idea had warped out of all recognition. Google may talk about democratization of information, but in the case of the book project, they own and control the information. It is made available to everyone under the terms they want.

Much like the worries surrounding Streetview, the book project and the concerns from authors have largely faded from public view. 11 years after the Author's Guild launched the first legal action, the US Supreme Court declined to consider an appeal against the last ruling which went in Google's favor.

The authors of creative works can, it seems, no longer expect to be in control of their own work once it is released in to the world. If music is uploaded onto YouTube by a fan, it will remain there. If a book is scanned, there is little chance of ever getting it removed. This democratization of information is quickly coming to mean that the biggest companies are able to take whatever they want under the guise of making it accessible to all.

With libraries under threat in most countries, there is a real danger that information, instead of being freely available to all, will instead be a resource tightly controlled by an extremely small number of entities across the planet.

Google has stuck by the book project for practically the whole life of the company, demonstrating how close to their hearts the founders hold it. The company is far less emotionally attached to the dozens of other projects it cancels every year, many of which never come close to being released into the world. These 'moonshot' projects cost Google $895m in the first quarter of 2016. The bulk of this money goes on things like the self-driving cars, which are still some way from showing a profit. Other areas of interest for the company are putting giant balloons into the air to bring Internet access to remote areas (Project Loom), having drone aircraft zipping between the balloons delivering stuff (Project Wing), robots (Project Replicant), more drones (Project Titan) a bionic contact lens and general human immortality.

3.5 Conclusion

There will never be a complete history of the Internet written. Even if it morphs beyond all recognition, it will always be some a globe-spanning structure which allows anyone to venture in and move around. The underlying technology will undoubtedly change but so quickly has the developed world become reliant on seamless communication between disparate groups of people that it is difficult to imagine a scenario in which we ever decide to switch the whole thing off.

The speed of change may increase, both as new generations of users build on and improve what exists today and as new technology springs to life, as seemingly far off now as smartphones were only 20 years ago. Truly intelligent artificial intelligence may be just around the corner, and computing power may reach astronomical levels with the arrival of quantum based-systems.

We have little reason to think that things will ever plateau, progress is under threat of halting more due to our own short-sightedness than any natural limitation. For technology to continue to march on, more advances must be made in the safe production and disposal of the sea of gadgets which currently rely on slave labor for the mining of raw materials and which are ultimately dumped on Third World countries. Steps should be taken to reduce dependency on rare-earth minerals, the supply of which may be more strictly controlled by a few countries in the future.

Importantly, governments should stop reacting to each new service and try instead to pre-empt things which may affect the voting public. By working more closely with the people setting out to make big changes, the population as a whole will be shielded from the whims of those with ideas and money and we may see more commonly useful things being brought to the marketplace. We should not allow ourselves to feel that we must be at the mercy of those whose dreams and ambitions are used to justify massive, ultimately selfish upsets to a status quo which may be more beneficial to a greater number of people.

Above all, people must realize that even in this hyper-technological time, they still have a choice and it is important that the choice remains, even if few choose to exercise it. We should never allow ourselves to become dependent on or forced to use products or services in order to carry out our daily lives. These things may make the process easier or cheaper or more efficient, but they should never be mandatory.

Technology is cold and emotionless and logical, but the people who make it aren't, despite what they would like to think. Everything created by humans will be shaped and tempered by the same prejudices and irrationality displayed by everyone walking the planet. Technology gives us the means to achieve more than we are naturally capable of; this has been true since the first stone struck the first hard nut. The amplification of our ability extends to all our facets, good and bad.

About

Gareth Little is former tech-enthusiast turned skeptic. Originally from Scotland, he moved to Japan after leaving the Royal Air Force and qualifying as an ethical computer hacker and encryption specialist. 'They're Coming for You' is his first work.

www.garethalittle.com
Twitter @garethalittle

www.ingramcontent.com/pod-product-compliance
Lightning Source LLC
Chambersburg PA
CBHW061436180526
45170CB00004B/1433